# GLOBETR

## *Travel*

# FLORIDA

LIZ BOOTH

NEW
HOLLAND

NEW
HOLLAND

★★★ Highly recommended
★★ Recommended
★ See if you can

Fourth edition published in 2005
by New Holland Publishers (UK) Ltd
London • Cape Town • Sydney • Auckland
First published in 1997
10 9 8 7 6 5 4 3 2 1
www.newhollandpublishers.co.za

Garfield House, 86 Edgware Road
London W2 2EA, United Kingdom

80 McKenzie Street
Cape Town, 8001
South Africa

14 Aquatic Drive
Frenchs Forest, NSW 2086
Australia

218 Lake Road
Northcote, Auckland
New Zealand

Distributed in the USA by
The Globe Pequot Press, Connecticut

ISBN 1 84537 004 X

**Keep us Current**
Information in travel guides is apt to change, which is
why we regularly update our guides. We'd be grateful
to receive feedback if you've noted something we
should include in our updates. If you have new
information, please share it with us by writing to the
Publishing Manager, Globetrotter, at the office nearest
to you (addresses on this page). The most significant
contribution to each new edition will receive a free
copy of the updated guide.

**Publishing Manager (UK):** Simon Pooley
**Publishing Manager (SA):** Thea Grobbelaar
**DTP Cartographic Manager:** Genené Hart
**Editors:** Melany McCallum, Tarryn Berry, Mary Duncan,
Claudia Dos Santos
**Cartographers:** Nicole Engeler, William Smuts
**Design and DTP:** Sonya Cupido
**Compiler:** Elaine Fick

Reproduction by Hirt & Carter (Pty) Ltd, Cape Town.
Printed and bound by Times Offset (M) Sdn. Bhd.,
Malaysia.

**Photographic Credits:**
**Astronaut Memorial Planetarium**, p. 66; **Jon Davison**, pp. 7,
9 (bottom), 11 (bottom), 18, 94, 95; **Nicole Engeler**, p. 59;
**Chris Fairclough Colour Library**, pp. 88, 93 (bottom),
106; **Henry Morrison Flagler Museum**, p. 15; **Florida
Division of Tourism**, p. 96; **Fort Myers Historical
Museum**, p. 10; **Hutchison Library/J Henderson**, p. 117;
**Hutchison Library/Dr Nigel Smith**, p. 12; **Hutchison
Library/Tony Souter**, pp. 49, 75; **International Photo-
bank**, cover; **Kravis Cultural Center**, p. 22; **Life File/
Emma Lee**, pp. 14, 20, 100, 108; **Life File/ R Williamson**,
p. 116; **Museum of Man in the Sea**, p. 93; **P Murphy**,
pp. 13, 57, 80; **Photobank/Adrian Baker**, pp. 4, 26, 30, 50
(used with permission from Disney Enterprises, Inc.), 53,
103 (bottom), 104; **Photobank/Peter Baker**, pp. 19, 27,
28, 29 (bottom); **Photobank/Gary Goodwin**, pp. 46, 52;
**PictureBank Photo Library Ltd**, pp. 17, 35 (top), 62, 69;
**Ponce Inlet Lighthouse Association**, p. 73; **Marjorie
Kinnan Rawlings State Historic Site**, p. 85; **Neil
Setchfield**, p. 58; **Jeroen Snijders**, pp. 11 (top), 21, 33,
36–40, 42, 43, 67, 68, 70, 78, 81, 83, 90–92, 97, 107, 109;
**Spectrum Colour Library**, pp. 71, 115; **Travel Ink/Abbie
Enock**, pp. 23, 35 (bottom), 103 (top), 118; **University of
Florida**, Harn Museum of Art, p. 84; **Visit USA Associa-
tion**, pp. 25, 41; **Lawson Wood**, pp. 9 (top), 112, 114, 119;
**Zefa**, pp. 6, 8, 16, 24, 29 (top), 54, 55, 65 (bottom), 82;
**Zefa/Armstrong**, title page; **Zefa/E G Carle**, p. 65 (top);
**Zefa/Damm**, p. 72; **Zefa/David Madison**, pp. 56, 74.

**Cover:** *Miami Beach coastline.*
**Title page:** *Miami, heart of the cruise-ship industry.*

# CONTENTS

# 1
# Introducing Florida

Flanked by the Atlantic Ocean and the Gulf of Mexico, crisscrossed by rivers and streams and dotted with lakes, Florida is dominated by water. This abundance has not only shaped the landscape, but provided a perfect playground for citizens and tourists alike.

Discover urban chic, glamour and glitz in **Miami** or head to **Orlando** and the spectacular wonders of **Walt Disney World**, seek out the vibrance of the **Keys** or the rolling white beaches out west. Indulge in the colonial history of the former regional capitals: **Pensacola** in the northwest and **St Augustine** on the east coast. Today's state capital, **Tallahassee**, lies in the centre of the northern region, nominated as a compromise between feuding east and west coast settlers. Sprawling **Jacksonville** provides a gateway for travellers heading south from the eastern seaboard of the United States, and areas like **Daytona Beach** swarm with American visitors each spring.

Those in need of quiet will welcome the sunsets and the scenery. For nature lovers there is the hushed mystery of the **Everglades** and the underwater extravaganza of the **Florida Keys**. Snorkelling and diving are encouraged particularly in the **John Pennekamp Coral Reef State Park** in the Keys, and at **Peacock Springs State Park** at Luraville where certified divers can explore some of the 28,000ft (8500m) of surveyed caves.

For families Florida is hard to beat with its choice of theme parks from Walt Disney World to **Busch Gardens** and **Universal Orlando**, as well as many safe beaches and a wide range of family-orientated hotels and restaurants.

### TOP ATTRACTIONS

**\*\*\* Walt Disney World:** sensational entertainment.
**\*\*\* Universal Orlando:** a movie wonderland.
**\*\*\* NASA Kennedy Visitor Complex:** launch base for the space shuttles.
**\*\*\* Everglades:** beautiful natural wonderland.
**\*\*\* South Beach Miami:** vibrant Art Deco district.
**\*\*\* Key West:** unique island and yachting lifestyle.
**\*\*\* St Augustine:** wealth of history in the oldest city in Florida.

**Opposite:** *Sailing, one of the attractions at St Pete Beach on the West Coast.*

**Above:** *The Everglades flow hundreds of miles, creating shady swamps that shelter alligators and other wildlife.*

## THE LAND

Geologists estimate that Florida is one of the very youngest parts of the continental United States and the last land mass to have emerged from the primordial ocean. This is a low-lying region, generally less than 100ft (30m) above sea level. The highest point, at just 345ft (105m), lies in Walton County. Nowhere in Florida is more than 60 miles (100km) from a beach.

The 450,000-acre (182,112ha) **Lake Okeechobee** is the state's largest freshwater area. It feeds into the Everglade Basin, which stretches for many miles with water just a few inches deep. Strictly speaking, this is really a slow-moving river, 150 miles (240km) long and 50 miles (80km) wide. Now a protected territory, the river-cum-swamp provides a safe haven for about 300 different species of bird, some 600 kinds of fish and a number of animals, like the rare Florida panther.

To the north Florida is dominated by great **hardwood forests** and vast open tracts of beautiful beach. The **Suwannee River** flows 177 miles (283km) and is fed by more than 20 major springs before reaching the **Gulf of Mexico**. Green, rolling hills and large pine forests dominate the northwest **Panhandle**. This beautiful area, which is edged by salt marshes and expansive, sparkling-white sand beaches has been nicknamed **The Emerald Coast**.

The deep, lush tropical forests and crystal waters of the **Florida Keys** remain a haven of peace and quiet and are perfect for exciting deep-water game fishing, coral reef diving and swimming. The string of islands curves 192 miles (309km) southwest from the mainland culminating in **Loggerhead Key** in the **Dry Tortugas**, although most people consider Key West to be the end of the line, because that's where the road ends.

## Climate

Florida earns its epithet The Sunshine State with hot
summers, punctuated by tropical storms and often hurricanes. This area experiences more thunderstorms than
any other part of the USA, the lightning causing numerous fires. Winters are generally warmer than in much of
the United States and Europe.

The state can be divided into two climatic zones –
**tropical** to the south of a line from Bradenton to Vero
Beach and **subtropical** to the north. Average annual
summer **temperatures** are 26.9°C (80.5°F) in the northern, and 55.1°C (82.7°F) in the southern regions. These
fall each winter to about 11.7°C (53°F) in the north and
20.3°C (68.5°F) in the south.

There are however notable exceptions. Winter tourists
are sometimes dismayed at the sight of **frost** as far south
as Miami, though this phenomenon is rare and usually
occurs in conjunction with blizzards or extremely low
temperatures on the northeast-
ern seaboard. The Keys have
never experienced frost.

Summer often brings **tropical
storms** and the state averages
53in (135cm) of rain a year. This
varies from about 40in (100cm)
in Key West to 62in (157cm) in
West Palm Beach. **Hurricanes**
can occur from June to
November but are most likely
in September. Their move-
ments are constantly
monitored and the state has
an established evacuation
programme. Hurricanes
can hit anywhere along the
coast, though the worst is
usually over within 24
hours, with bad weather
following the main storm
for several days afterwards.

**Below:** *Miles of white
sand beaches, like Bahia
Honda, line Florida's coast.*

| COMPARATIVE CLIMATE CHART | MIAMI | | | | ORLANDO | | | | PENSACOLA | | | |
|---|---|---|---|---|---|---|---|---|---|---|---|---|
| | WIN | SPR | SUM | AUT | WIN | SPR | SUM | AUT | WIN | SPR | SUM | AUT |
| | JAN | APR | JULY | OCT | JAN | APR | JULY | OCT | JAN | APR | JULY | OCT |
| AVERAGE TEMP. °C | 15 | 20 | 24 | 22 | 8 | 17 | 23 | 19 | 12 | 20 | 27 | 21 |
| AVERAGE TEMP. °F | 67 | 75 | 82 | 79 | 49 | 63 | 75 | 67 | 53 | 67 | 81 | 70 |
| HOURS OF SUN | 12 | 13 | 14 | 12 | 12 | 13 | 14 | 12 | 12 | 13 | 14 | 12 |
| RAINFALL mm | 51 | 76 | 152 | 179 | 53 | 55 | 197 | 71 | 109 | 109 | 177 | 99 |
| RAINFALL in | 2 | 3 | 6 | 7 | 2 | 2 | 8 | 3 | 4.5 | 4.5 | 7 | 4 |
| DAYS OF RAINFALL | 7 | 8 | 12 | 13 | 7 | 7 | 14 | 9 | 9 | 9 | 12 | 9 |

**MANGROVE FORESTS**

Florida is home to the red, white, black and buttonwood mangroves.
**Red mangroves:** found nearest the ocean, they survive by supporting themselves on prop roots that arch deep into the ground. They provide vital nursery grounds for young reptiles, fish and birds.
**White mangroves:** prefer higher ground and grow further inland, often forming hummocks with larger land-based trees such as mahogany and gumbo-limbo.
**Black mangroves:** identified by the short, finger-like roots that are used as airways and burst out of the ground all around the tree.
**Buttonwood mangroves:** are very similar to the white mangroves, also preferring higher ground.

## Plant Life

Florida's sandy loam and peat ground are just two of 300 local soil types, making this one of the most fertile areas in the United States. The state is home to over 300 tree species and more than 3500 other plants. **Mangrove**, **cypress**, **palm**, **pine** and **oak** are predominant. Species like **maple** and **magnolia** are found mainly in the north.

Vast **grasslands** are found across the state, forming large, lush prairies which sustain vast herds of cattle. A unique **scrubland** covers much of the dry, sandy coasts. The freshwater and coastal **swamps** abound with trees, grasses and flowers, which provide a rich breeding ground for wildlife.

Florida is home to three diverse national forests: **Apalachicola** (hardwood/pine as well as carnivorous plants), **Osceola** (cypress swamps) and **Ocala** (desert scrub), which combined cover more than 1,000,000 acres (404,695ha) yet would all fit inside the sweeping expanse of the **Everglades National Park**. The state also offers some unusual marine parks, including the 175,000-acre (70,821ha) **Biscayne National Park** southeast of Miami

which is renowned for its many shipwrecks (some dating back to the pirate days of the 16th century) the **John Pennekamp Coral Reef State Park** around Key Largo which offers divers a close-up view of living reefs, and the wildlife sanctuary **Dry Tortugas**, west of Key West. In total the state maintains some 156 parks.

Only some 40% of the land is used for agriculture, with one-third of that set aside for timber or pasture. The farmland, however, is very productive and Florida is known for its **citrus groves**, which produce about three-quarters of all the fruit sold in the entire United States. The state is second only to California in terms of vegetable production.

## Wildlife

While probably most famous for its '**gators**', Florida also has more than 400 types of **bird**, some 100 different species of mammal, and over 700 varieties of fish. **Panthers**, sadly, are on the endangered list, which also includes puma, boar and black bears; but rehabilitation programmes

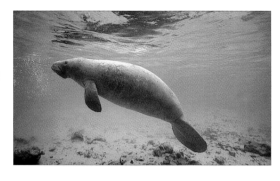

underway at national parks throughout the state are proving successful in halting the decline of Florida's interesting fauna.

Out at sea there is a variety of dolphins and porpoises as well as the **manatee**, or sea-cow. Manatees, once hunted to the brink of extinction for their meat, hide and oil, are now the object of a dedicated protection programme. The world of **fish** is fascinating, yielding more kinds here than anywhere else in the world, from grouper, snapper and flounder to tarpon, marlin and shark. Fishing is permitted in 35 of the Florida State Parks (www.floridastateparks.org)

Swimming in the Everglades is not recommended due to a large population of deceptively docile **alligators**. Many golf courses sport alligator warning signs at their water hazards.

Florida's climate is also enjoyed by some 40 species of snake, including venomous varieties such as two kinds of **rattlesnake** and the **copperhead**. The **coral snake** and the water- or **cottonmouth moccasin** are potentially lethal, but you are more likely to encounter them behind glass in wildlife parks than slithering around outdoors.

More than 400 species of bird either live in or migrate to Florida – the coastal areas often form breeding sites for thousands of seabirds. **Bald eagles** and **turkeys** can sometimes be spotted inland and Florida houses the largest breeding colonies of egrets, herons, ibises and pelicans north of the Caribbean. In the Everglades you may be lucky enough to spot the rare **purple gallinule**.

**Above:** *Manatees were thought to be mermaids by the sailors of earlier centuries.*
**Opposite:** *Florida's citrus fruit is the agricultural mainstay of the region.*
**Below:** *The beautiful and rare purple gallinule.*

**TRAIL ETIQUETTE**

- Carry away all your rubbish.
- Don't feed the animals!
- Stay on designated trails.
- Extinguish all camp fires (where permitted) after use.
- Don't bring pets into parks.
- Beware of hunting seasons.
- Avoid shining torches at nesting turtles.

## HISTORY IN BRIEF
### Native Americans

The earliest inhabitants, native Americans travelling from the frigid north, discovered balmy Florida about 12,000 years ago. Awaiting them was a land of plenty teeming with wildlife and fish. Little evidence has been found to suggest that they were more than **hunter-gatherers**.

Primitive irrigation ditches indicate that the first farming communities existed around 500BC, although their southern Florida counterparts remained hunter-gatherers until the arrival of the Europeans. Unfortunately, many of the priceless ancient burial mounds and artefacts have been destroyed in the continuous quest for modern housing and development.

### European Settlers

Florida first appears on a crude Spanish map of 1502 and a few years later was described as the 'Land of Eternal Youth' by European explorers. But it was Spaniard **Juan Ponce de León** who really discovered Florida for the Europeans in 1513. Travelling north from the established Puerto Rico, he was searching for the mythical **Fountain**

---

**JUAN PONCE DE LEÓN**

Juan Ponce de León landed in 1513 somewhere between the St Johns River and St Augustine, after mistaking the land for the Bahamas. He then sailed south around the coast, before returning to the Caribbean where he was governor of Puerto Rico. However, Juan Ponce de León was a man with a mission. He had been entrusted by the King of Spain to find the isle of Bimini, home of the fabled Fountain of Eternal Youth, and to search for gold. Having failed to find gold in Puerto Rico, stories of untold wealth lured him north. His life's mission came to an abrupt end during a later stay in Florida when he was severely wounded by a Calusa Indian arrow and taken back to Puerto Rico, where he died.

**of Youth**. Juan Ponce de León waded ashore on the northeast coast, somewhere near today's St Augustine, and named the land '**La Florida**' in honour of the Spanish Easter Festival of Flowers, *Pascua Florida,* that had just been celebrated aboard his ship.

Believing Florida to be no more than an island in the Bahamas, it was a further eight years before he returned to establish a colony in the Fort Myers area. But he and his men were then savagely attacked by hostile Calusa Indians. The opinion today is that the Calusas had been forewarned by their island cousins from Puerto Rico and Haiti, who had been subjected to hardship and slavery by the Spanish overlords. De León was wounded and fled back to Cuba where he died.

The next European foray into the region occurred seven years later in 1528. Lured by tales of untold treasure, another Spaniard, **Panfilo de Narváez**, landed at Tampa Bay with over 400 men. His plan was to discover how Florida connected to Mexico, but the expedition took its toll and a further eight years went by before just four of the original party managed to find their way there.

In 1559 **Tristan de Luna y Arellano** founded a colony in Pensacola Bay with 1400 pioneers; it failed two years later when the settlement was destroyed by a hurricane. However, it was revived 139 years later and on the strength of this argument the people of today's Pensacola claim to live in Florida's oldest town – a fact hotly disputed by the residents of St Augustine where a colony was established in 1565 by **Pedro Menéndez de Avilés**. He used this new town as a base from which to attack Fort Caroline, which had been set up by the French Huguenots and was seen as a threat to Spanish shipping lanes.

**Above:** *Pedro Menéndez de Avilés was one of the first Europeans to set foot in Florida.*
**Opposite:** *Calusa Indians at the time of arrival of the European explorers.*
**Below:** *This lovely 12th-century monastery was transported from Spain and reconstructed in Florida.*

## HISTORICAL CALENDAR

**1497** Europeans see Florida for the first time and record it on maps.

**1513** Juan Ponce de León wades ashore and names the land 'La Florida' after the Spanish Festival of Flowers.

**1559** Tristan de Luna lands and settles at Pensacola, but is forced to withdraw two years later after a devastating hurricane.

**1565** Pedro Menéndez de Avilés founds the first settlement at St Augustine for Spanish King Philip II.

**1763** After a century of raids by native Americans, French and British, the Spanish relinquish Florida to England in exchange for Havana, Cuba.

**1783** British cede Florida back to the Spanish.

**1785** The start of three years' skirmishing between Spanish and American forces.

**1813–18** General Andrew Jackson enters western Florida to campaign against native Americans in three wars.

**17 July 1821** General Jackson receives Florida for the United States from the Spanish in a ceremony in Pensacola.

**1822** A Florida government is established under Governor William Duval.

**1836** The St Joseph to Lake Wimico rail track is the very first line to operate in the state of Florida.

**1842** The Second Seminole War ends with the transfer of nearly 4000 Seminole Indians to Arkansas and Oklahoma.

**1845** Florida officially becomes the 27th state of the United States with William D Moseley as governor.

**1855–58** The third and final Seminole Indian war takes place.

**1894** Henry Flagler completes railroad as far as Palm Beach.

**1958** National Aeronautics and Space Administration (NASA), starts work at Cape Canaveral.

**16 July 1969** The historic Apollo 11 mission lifts off from Cape Kennedy to carry the first men to the moon.

**1 October 1971** Walt Disney World opens the Magic Kingdom in Orlando.

**1981** The first manned space shuttle is launched from John F Kennedy Space Center.

**24 August 1992** Hurricane Andrew hits the east coast, destroying much of Homestead and South Dade County and causing the evacuation of thousands of residents.

**2000** By the turn of the new century, Florida's population had grown to almost 16 million, making it the fourth most populous in the US.

### Spanish Dominance

The Spanish retained control of Florida over almost two centuries despite constant warring with local Indians, the French from the Louisiana area and the British living in Carolina and Georgia. Towns were often under siege, and

St Augustine endured a 52-day attack on one occasion. Even **Sir Francis Drake** made his bid for Florida with a failed attack in 1586.

In 1763 the British forces gained control of Florida in a swap for Havana, Cuba, as part of the **Treaty of Paris**, the final settlement of the Seven Year War which had devastated Europe.

This ended military rule, with the army exchanged for civil servants. However, Florida did not remain British for long. It was used as a base against the colonists in the **American War of Independence**. After losing their battle, the British handed Florida back to Spain in return for the Bahamas.

### United States Control and the Seminole Wars

The new Americans and the Spanish Floridians constantly battled over the border. By this time the population of Florida included Africans, West Indians, Greeks, Germans and Sicilians among others. **General Andrew Jackson** from Tennessee finally swayed the balance by capturing Pensacola which led to Spain's cession of Florida to the United States on 17 July 1821.

By this time the various native American tribes were collectively known as the **Seminoles**, from *se-mi-no-lee* (a Creek word meaning 'runaway'). The reluctant Indians were hustled out of their territories and despatched unceremoniously; many fled and sought refuge in the forests and swamps, hence their name. The **First Seminole War** took place during 1817–18. A second war followed between 1835–42, culminating in the Removal Act which resulted in most of the Seminole Indians being sent off to Arkansas and Oklahoma.

**Tallahassee**, originally a native American village, was made the territory capital in 1824 to end arguments between Pensacola and St Augustine over which had the right to lead the region. Indians were not the only problem facing the settlers. St Joseph was a boom town in 1835, competing with nearby Apalachicola as a trading port. But the flourishing community of some 12,000 people vanished within nine years, the result of a deadly outbreak of yellow fever and a destructive hurricane.

**Above:** *Floridians are proud of their history and love to re-enact the past. Here a man is dressed like a 17th-century soldier at Castillo de San Marcos.* **Opposite:** *Castillo de San Marcos, a 17th-century Spanish castle and now one of the top attractions in St Augustine.*

**Right:** *Florida's citrus fruit is exported all over the world.*
**Opposite:** *Railroad king, Henry M Flagler, brought the first railway lines down to Miami and transformed the region.*

---

**PLIGHT OF THE NATIVE AMERICAN**

The arrival of Europeans in the 1500s forced the native Americans to fight for every inch of their ancestral land. By 1800, only a handful of the once proud **Tequesta** and **Calusa** Indian population remained alived.

At this time, **Creek** and **Muskogee** tribes, known collectively as Seminoles, were forced south by the encroaching development of the United States. They settled in Florida, raiding settlements and providing shelter for runaway slaves. Three wars followed, during which most Seminoles were killed or forcibly removed to reservations in Alabama and Oklahoma. Only about 150 hid deep in the swamps, forming the basis of the small community left today.

---

During the epidemic Apalachicola fared better, with some help from bank director and postmaster **John Gorrie** who was also a doctor. He treated his yellow fever sufferers by cooling their rooms, as it was believed at the time that malaria and other tropical diseases were caused by the hot sticky air of the swamps. John Gorrie did not live to see the eventual fruits of his research. Ridiculed in New York, he died a broken man survived by his invention: the forerunner of the fridge and of the air conditioner.

Florida became an American state in 1845 by which time only a few hundred Seminoles were left. A third and final war, sparked off by an unfortunate misunderstanding, erupted between 1855–58, leading to great loss of life before the proud native Americans finally had to concede defeat. A small number still live in the Everglades.

### Civil War

The battles of the **American Civil War** largely passed Florida by, although the state did supply the Confederate South with salt, beef and bacon and 15,000 troops. 1290 men joined the Union Army (the Yankee North) which captured several of Florida's seaports. Pensacola was one such city with the **Yankees** holding Fort Pickens and the **Confederacy** in control of Fort McRee. The southern rebels were the first to crack, fleeing the city in 1862. Fort Pickens escaped civil war skirmishes and became the area's first tourist attraction when the government imprisoned **Chief Geronimo** here in 1886. Crowds used to gather outside to see the Apache Indian in captivity.

## Railroad

The American railroad, which was having such an impact across the country, also affected Florida. The Tallahassee to St Marks railroad, conceived and financed by wealthy entrepreneurs from northern Florida who gradually opened up the southern end of the state – helped by the enthusiasm of existing residents – operated from 1837–84. Miami was first developed in the 1860s and 1870s but it was not until 1894, when local resident **Julia Tuttle** sent a fresh orange blossom north to railroad magnate **Henry M Flagler** in frosty Palm Beach to persuade him to bring the track all the way south, that things really started to happen.

Henry Flagler extended the Florida East Coast Railway down through the Florida Keys in 1912. Although the track was destroyed by the hurricane of 1935, the same path was followed during construction of the existing Overseas Highway.

The start of the tourist trade and the expansion of agriculture both date back to the railroad development of the late 1800s. Now, for the first time farmers could export their goods nationwide and visitors could take advantage of Florida's warm winters.

## Booming Miami

The original 'jetsetters' discovered Miami and the wonderful south early in the 20th century and a property boom followed (in the year 1925 alone, 481 hotels and apartments rose in Miami Beach). Devastating hurricanes in 1926 and 1935 failed to stop the flow of money into the

### THE CIVIL WAR YEARS

When Florida was at its peak as a plantation state some 39,000 out of a population of about 87,000 were slaves. The third state to join the pro-slavery **Confederate** cause, Florida seceded from the **Union** (the northern states) in 1861. It supplied food and arms to the cause as well as thousands of men – only 1290 of them joined the Union army. Although Union soldiers occupied most of the seaports to mount a blockade against the Confederacy, the state really only suffered two battles. In February 1864 the **Battle of Olustee**, near Live Oak, cost 300 lives with both sides claiming victory. The more decisive victory came at Tallahassee a year later when a group of raw recruits saved the capital from falling into the hands of the Union.

fledgling city and various events shaped and moulded its ambience. The famous Art Deco area of Miami was developed in 1930, while the 1960s saw the arrival of **Cubans** fleeing the revolutionary Fidel Castro.

Most of the Cuban refugees lived in temporary ghettos, but the failure of the 'Bay of Pigs' invasion of 1961 and the threatening Cuban Missile Crisis of 1962 convinced the growing exile community that it would be a long time before they could return home. With time they came to lend a strong new Latin-American flavour to Miami, now often considered the financial capital of the Caribbean and where English may appear to be a second language.

## Modern-day Florida

Further north the government was investing in outer space and the National Aeronautics and Space Administration (**NASA**) began operations at Cape Canaveral. The historic Apollo 11 mission was launched here on 16 July 1969, taking the first men to the moon. Twelve years later the first space shuttle lifted off from the **John F Kennedy Space Center**.

**Below:** *A space shuttle blasts off from the John F Kennedy Space Center.*

The state has continued to develop rapidly and although recession has slowed the property boom, thousands of older people still make Florida their retirement home and plenty of others are still immigrating to the state; jointly, tourism and agriculture remain its most valuable industries. By 2002 the population of Florida had grown to an estimated 16.7 million, making it the fourth most populated state in the United States after California, New York and Texas.

But the influx of people has a downside too since many of the refugees, now especially from Haiti, are poorly educated and unskilled, thereby placing enormous strain on the social aid institutions.

# GOVERNMENT AND ECONOMY

The state government was formally established in 1885, although it has been modified frequently since then. The most recent changes occurred in 1968 when the electorate approved 20 revisions to the constitution.

Florida is ruled by a **governor** and **lieutenant governor** (these two candidates run as a team during elections), as well as six **cabinet members** – a secretary of state, attorney general, treasurer, comptroller and commissioners of education and agriculture.

The Executive is supported by a **Senate** of 40 and the **House of Representatives** with 120 members. Florida tends to be dominated by the **Democrats** in both its state legislature and those serving in the **United States Congress**. Conversely, Floridians tend to vote Republican for their governors and in presidential elections. Florida became the controversial hotseat in the last race for the White House with both the Democrats and Republicans claiming victory, before taking to the law courts where the Republicans eventually took victory.

Florida has a number of constitutional prohibitions and **tax** exemptions. There is no personal income tax or inheritance tax on homesteads; instead the state relies on corporate tax and a general 'sales and use' tax, which accounts for over half of the revenue.

## Economic Development

Throughout the 1800s Florida's rapid economic development mirrored the expansion of the railroad system. Until 1821 the entire region was little more than an unexploited backwater, then the railroad magnates began to look further south, thereby prompting industrial growth.

### TIME TO CHANGE

Florida has two time zones – Eastern Standard and Central Standard Time. The state is located in the south rather than the east but such was the power of the railroad magnates, that it was included in Eastern Standard Time in order to make the rail timetables more convenient. Eastern Standard Time is five hours behind Greenwich Mean Time, while the area to the west of the Apalachicola River is on Central Standard Time, six hours behind GMT. The United States has instituted Daylight Saving in the summer, bringing clocks forward by one hour.

**Below:** *Florida is governed from the Senate House in Tallahassee.*

**Above:** *Miami has become the regional hub for cruises throughout the Caribbean.*

The original industries, **agriculture** and **tourism**, still dominate. Even today, enduring development and success depends heavily on a reliable transport network. Railroads continue to play an important part, though air travel has improved east–west links like those from Miami to Tampa.

Miami International Airport is a major hub for the region, serving not only Europe but the Caribbean and Latin America, while Orlando is developing its international links, particularly in the charter market.

Roads play an even greater role and a network of highways links most of the major centres. The **Overseas Highway** is the main access route into the Florida Keys for most tourist traffic.

With so much coastline, **shipping** is vital and the state boasts eight deep-water ports and more than 994 miles (1600km) of navigable waterways.

### Tourism and Agriculture

Tourism is the state's largest industry and, despite a dip in the early 1990s, has been growing steadily for the past decade. In 2003 a record 74.5 million tourists visited the state. About 83% of visitors are United States citizens, with most international visitors hailing from Canada, Germany and the UK. In 2002, tourism generated $50.86bn for the state.

Florida provides the United States with 75% of its **citrus fruit** and is second only to California in vegetable production, with **tomatoes** the leading crop. The state also provides about 40% of the nation's **sugar cane**, as well as greenhouse and foliage plants. **Timber** is harvested in the north while the southern and central grasslands sustain the state's livestock and thoroughbred racehorses.

## THE PEOPLE

Despite a comparatively slow start, Florida's population boomed during the 20th century and is today the fourth largest in the United States with some 16.7 million residents. People are concentrated mainly in the **urban belts** with vast areas of the state relatively untouched.

Floridians represent a rich cultural mix of racial and ethnic groups, each lending their special character, colour and spirit. The official language is English, though in some sections of Miami Spanish prevails. Place names have been influenced by both the original native American inhabitants and the Spanish.

### Native Americans

The arrival of Europeans during the 16th century left the native American population decimated by disease, slavers, land disputes and wars. By the time the United States gained control, only some 5000 **Seminoles** remained – three wars had sealed the fate of an entire tribe. Many were relocated to Arkansas and Oklahoma; a final 150 fled deep into the Everglades, eking out an existence with fishing and hunting while modern development changed their ancestral land.

The past few years have seen a change in attitude towards native Americans, who at last have been accorded the deserved respect. Today the descendants of the original native Americans live in three **reservations** in southern Florida (Big Cypress, Miccosukee and Seminole Indian Reserve); here they use their knowledge of the Glades as a way of earning money. You can take a trip into the swamps accompanied by a Seminole guide and experience a fascinating glimpse of Indian life in one of the nearby villages, where traditional craftwork is continued and gripping dances are put on for the benefit of visitors.

> **STEAMING AHEAD**
>
> Florida plans to be among the first US states to have a high-speed rail network, which ultimately would cut journey times between Miami and Orlando to around 82 minutes. The network would also include Tampa and would have stops at international airports to give visitors easy access around the state. So far the ambitious project has been stalled by issues with government funding although two most favoured consortiums have been identified for the project.

**Below:** *A native American guide navigates an airboat tour through the Everglades.*

They are a proud people coming to terms with past injustices, poverty and hardship, in an effort to reclaim their rightful place in modern Florida without losing touch with their ancient heritage and customs.

### The African-Americans

After the United States won control of Florida in1821, white planters began to develop massive plantations, relying on slave labour. Large numbers of Africans were forcibly shipped in to man these new plantations and citrus groves, and by the 1830s the white and black communities were of approximately equal size, number-ing some 11,000 each. This balance continued right up until the abolition of slavery – a federal census of 1860 found 62,000 black slaves within a population of 140,000. Although sparsely populated southern parts of Florida offered refuge for runaway slaves, northern Florida remained for a long time the deepest of the Deep South, both socially and politically. Slavery was, in principle, ended by the Civil War, but the agricultural patterns of Florida stayed ingrained for another fifty years.

Eventually the arrival of tourism offered opportunities for African-Americans, though it was not until the 1964 Civil Rights Act that wider based civil liberty could be guaranteed. Today, African-Americans form a smaller proportion of the population, outnumbered by the influx of white migrants that has taken place since the 1900s.

**Below:** *Tourists flock to admire the view from Sunset Pier, Key West.*
**Opposite:** *Cubans started arriving in large numbers in Florida in the 1960s.*

### Senior Citizens

Florida's demographic statis-tics changed dramatically with the arrival of the 'blue-rinse brigade' in the early 20th century. Numbers of white residents climbed rapidly as retirees from the northern states recognized that Florida winters were much kinder on old bones. Now every year thousands of senior citizens choose to retire in the sun and come to Florida. Although retirees came to dominate Miami Beach, in particular, from the 1970s, many new arrivals opt for Florida's small rural towns thereby contributing to a drop in the average age of beach city residents.

## The Cubans

Although the Fidel Castro-led 1959 **revolution in Cuba** was initially popular, many Cubans became disillusioned as the new regime became increasingly authoritarian. Between 1965 and 1973, 230,000 arrived in Miami on the so-called 'freedom fights' from Havana, joining the 50,000 or so Cubans already in the city. Most settled along SW Eighth Street, soon better-known by its Spanish name, Calle Ocho, forming the core of what became **Little Havana**. Steady upward mobility has seen Cuban-Americans become highly influential in Miami life, and in shaping US-Cuban relations.

Most Cubans in Florida still live in and around the Miami area, contributing to the tangible Spanish feel of a city where English often seems to be a second language. Yet the community of Dade County successfully vetoed a move to have Miami declared officially bilingual. At **carnival** time, Calle Ocho in Little Havana comes alive to the throbbing sounds of Cuban music, the fragrant smell of Cuban cigars and the exuberant, vivid colours of the costumes.

## Art and Culture

Although the state of Florida is little over 170 years old it has a remarkable diversity of art and culture. Much of its history is on display and a willingness to preserve the past has ensured that attractions are easily accessible to visitors.

**Sarasota** has become the nerve centre of Florida's traditional arts. This central western town was home to the flamboyant circus master **John Ringling**, who lovingly built a 30-room Venetian-style mansion as a gift for his wife before splashing out another fortune on the

---

### PUBLIC HOLIDAYS

**1 January** • New Year's Day
**15 January** •
Martin Luther King's Birthday
**3rd Monday in February** •
Presidents Day
**Last Monday in May** •
Memorial Day
**4 July** • Independence Day
**1st Monday in September** •
Labor Day
**2nd Monday in October** •
Columbus Day
**11 November** •
Veteran's Day
**Last Thursday in November** •
Thanksgiving Day
**25 December** •
Christmas Day
Americans generally have less holiday than Europeans, with only a day off at Christmas and Easter. October 31 (**Halloween**) is almost a holiday, with kids 'trick or treating', nowadays usually by car for safety.

**Above:** *Florida prides itself on its arts and culture. The Kravis Cultural Center in West Palm Beach is one of the leading venues.*

**John and Mable Ringling Museum of Art**, which now contains the world's finest collection of works by Flemish artist Rubens, and again on the **Circus Museum**, filled with memorabilia from The Greatest Show on Earth. Don't miss the state's only 18th-century Italian theatre, the **Asolo Theater,** and its Center for the Performing Arts, dismantled in Italy, and shipped and reassembled in Florida in the 1950s.

Nearby **Tampa** has one of only four museums in the country dedicated exclusively to African-American Art. Also in Tampa is an interesting Museum of Art with seven galleries of Greek and Roman antiquities, plus the **Tampa Bay Performing Arts Center**. Most other cities in the state boast a harmonious variety of art and history museums as well as some rather uncommon establishments. Be sure to visit the Underwater Demolition Team **SEAL** (Sea, Air and Land) **Museum** in Fort Pierce, which was a training site for navy divers in 1943, and the **American Police Hall of Fame** and Museum in Miami.

For historical interest the spotlight has to fall on **Pensacola** and **St Augustine**, the two cities vying for the right to the title 'Oldest in Florida'. Both boast numerous museums with captivating exhibitions as well as lovingly preserved historical areas to substantiate their respective claims. Visit Seville, Palafox and the North Hill Preservation District of Pensacola or see The Old Jail, The Oldest House, the Oldest Store Museum and the Oldest Wooden Schoolhouse, all in St Augustine, which also offers a restored Spanish Quarter complete with costumed guides and a daily re-enactment of life 400 years ago. On the third Saturday night in June each year a torchlit procession winds its way through St Augustine's old quarter, part of a Spanish Night Watch festival.

*Left: A mural in Ybor City, the Cuban heartland on the West Coast.*

Though Florida escaped most of the horrors of the Civil War, some events are remembered annually, such as the **Battle of Natural Bridge** at which the Confederacy managed to save Tallahassee from falling into the hands of the Union forces. Each February some 2000 volunteers in full uniform relive the battle at **Lake City**. A month later the soldiers are out in force again some 62 miles (100km) to the west, to commemorate the **Battle of Olustee**.

Of Florida's countless festivals the **Art Deco Weekend Festival** in Miami Beach and the **Hemingway Festival** on Key West are probably the best known. **Carnaval Miami**, held each March, is an introduction to the Hispanic culture of the city, while Jacksonville, Hollywood and Pensacola all feature large jazz festivals.

## Sports

In the Sunshine State the emphasis is on outdoor life with a dazzling array of sports facilities and outdoor activities. Camping in national parks, barbecuing in the backyard and volleyball on the beach have become an integral part of Florida's culture. The sun shines year-round and almost every sport has a place on the calendar.

Traditional American sports such as **baseball** and **American football** are well represented and you'll stumble into **basketball** and **volleyball** nets and goals on almost every beach and in many parks.

**Tennis** facilities still manage to outnumber golf courses, with more than 7700 around the state. These vary from a court alongside a hotel or park to upmarket Key Biscayne in Miami with its championship courts.

**National football league** teams include the Miami Dolphins, the Tampa Bay Buccaneers and the Jacksonville Jaguars. The **National Basketball Association** is represented by the Miami Heat and Orlando Magic teams while the **Major league baseball** teams include the Florida Marlins. **National hockey league** teams are the Florida Panthers and Tampa Bay Lightning.

**Motor-sport** enthusiasts should head for Daytona or Sebring for the Daytona 500 and endurance racing. **Horse racing** takes place in Gulfstream Park and the Pompano Harness Track offers trotting races, including the Breeders' Crown with its US$1 million prize money.

### Fishing and Water Sports

Water sports are split between fresh and salt, in and on! **Fishermen** have the choice of more than 7700 lakes, covering a total of 10 acres, as well as 1350 miles (2173km) of coastline. Deep-sea and big game fishing is an exciting option and day charters are widely available.

For water lovers there is the choice between surfing at Daytona Beach, snorkelling off the Florida Keys or scuba diving in natural caves. **Sailing**, **windsurfing** and **water-skiing** are offered around the coast as well as on the larger lakes, while **canoeing** has become a popular holiday in its own right as visitors explore the water-ways, especially in winter when there are no tropical storms and the mosquito plague is not so intense. Greater Fort Lauderdale claims to be the **yachting** capital of the world with more than 42,000 vessels registered locally.

**Below:** *Yacht Race Week off Key West attracts hundreds of participants.*

Swimmers have an overwhelming range of stunning beaches to choose from, as well as many lakes and rivers. Note that **swimming** is not recommended in the Everglades where you may suddenly be joined by a devoted 'gator. Most of the beaches have lifeguards who will readily advise on safety or changing weather conditions. Fort Lauderdale has the **International Swimming Hall of Fame**, complete with training facilities for swimmers and divers.

**Above:** *Palm Beach Golf Course is one of the 1100 courses across the state.*

## Golf

Florida boasts 1370 of the more than 14,000 golf courses in the United States. Tournaments take place throughout the year and a number of courses can be booked via tour operators before you depart from your home country.

Many courses, like the **Innisbrook Hilton** at Tarpon Springs, form part of luxury resorts; of these, the **Boca Raton Resort and Club** is rated one of the top two golfing venues in the United States. An additional hazard in Florida are the alligators – heed the warning signs – which really do live in the waterways of some of the golf courses!

## Attractions

Florida could rightly claim to be the playground of the world, containing literally hundreds of theme parks and attractions. The range is broad, from quaint, old-world museums to technological marvels. Every city has its theme parks and tourist attractions but central Florida is probably the heart of the industry.

The theme park industry is so prized that the state has its own **Florida Attraction Association** providing information on the top venues. Each attraction is constantly upgraded and millions of dollars are spent on sensational new rides.

### JAI ALAI

Introduced into Miami by the Cubans, this game originated in the **Basque** region of Spain. It is played in a 176ft (53m) walled court called a *fronton*. The players (*pelotaris*), wearing basket-like gloves called *cestas*, hurtle balls (*pelotas*) around the court at lightning speeds of up to 170mph (275kph) while spectators bet on the winning order. Courts exist in Fort Lauderdale, West Palm Beach, Orlando, Ocala and Daytona Beach. But the oldest *fronton*, built in 1926, is in Miami, where matches are played daily.

**Above:** *The spectacular water-ski display at Sea World, Orlando, is a favourite with spectators.*

Young and old want to meet Mickey Mouse – the massive **Walt Disney World Resort** proved to be so successful that it spawned a veritable explosion of neighbouring parks, capable of filling a two-week holiday to capacity. The Disney Resort not only includes such delights as the Magic Kingdom and Epcot, but also Disney-Animal Kingdom, some fine hotels and five championship golf courses for tired dads.

The Attraction Association has a total of no less than 26 parks listed in central Florida, from **Adventure Island** and the lovely zoo at **Busch Gardens** in Tampa Bay to **Gatorland** and **King Henry's Feast** in Orlando. Parks range from historical **Medieval Times** to the excitement of **Wet 'n Wild**, where swimming is secondary and the Surge ride claims to be the longest and fastest water ride in the Southeast.

If you are a fan of outer space visit the fascinating **Kennedy Space Center Spaceport USA** where you'll be thrilled by movies of shuttle take-offs and landings and may even be lucky enough to witness a shuttle blasting into orbit. This is backed up by the **US Astronaut Hall of Fame** where visitors can try the full-scale orbiter mock-up, whirling centrifuge and flight simulators.

South Florida attractions are more water-orientated. The **Billie Swamp Safari** features Seminole Indian shows and tours through the swamps, **Fury Catamarans** sail daily to the reef around the Keys and the **Jungle Queen** claims 50 years of serving the best shrimp-barbecue dinners while cruising out of Miami.

The more mechanically-minded will be interested in the **Henry Morrison Flagler Museum** in Miami, which pays tribute to the admirable railroad magnate. There's also the **Miami Museum of Science and Space Transit Planetarium**, as well as the **Weeks Air Museum** which hosts spectacular air shows.

Northern Florida's attractions tend to be more historical in flavour: displays of quaint Victorian bric-a-brac and train rides through the fine old streets of St Augustine. Pensacola is home to the **National Museum of Naval Aviation** and St Augustine has the eerie **Potter's Wax Museum** where more than 170 figures are represented.

---

**WALT DISNEY WORLD**

• Employs more than 55,000 cast members during busy periods, making it the largest single-site employer in the US.
• Has a daily population of 200,000 people.
• More than 2600 couples get married here every year
• The 47-sq-mile (111km²) area cost Walt Disney US$6 million.
• Opened in 1971 and was the first theme park in the Orlando area
• Employs 650 full-time gardeners who plant three million new bedding plants every year and mow 2000 lawns and fairways three times a week.
• Has more than 800 hanging baskets in constant bloom.

---

## Shopping

An attraction in its own right, shopping in Florida is a must for any visitor. With prices approximately a third lower than in Europe, and huge ranges of stock, it's very difficult indeed to resist the gigantic shopping malls that cater for the masses.

**Below:** *Shopping is not limited to factory outlets – kiosks are equally popular.*

**Above:** *John's Pass waterfront promises an entertaining afternoon.*

Even those with just a few hours in transit at Miami International Airport can catch a cab (taxi) to one of the nearby shopping malls to pick up a few bargains. **Westland Mall, Bayside Marketplace, Dadeland Mall** and the **Falls Shopping Center** are all within easy reach of the airport and offer a stunning variety of goods.

Shopping assumes entertainment proportions at places like the **Fort Lauderdale Swap Shop** which lures young and old with fairground rides and circus performances, and **Old Town** in Kissimmee which has an antique carousel and Ferris wheel.

Speciality shops abound, but outlet malls such as the gigantic **Sawgrass Mills Mall** outside Fort Lauderdale have become big business in the past few years, offering clothing at less-than-retail prices.

### Food and Drink

The great attraction of eating out in Florida is the variety on offer and the cost. If you fancy a 'chilli dog' for breakfast, someone will be selling one. Equally, if you want a complete meal for less than US$15 it will be available somewhere – all you have to do is hunt it down.

Ethnic restaurants mingle with American diners, fast-food outlets and seafood eateries. As well as ensuring a delectable smorgasbord of **seafood**, Florida's extensive coastline has led to the establishment of numerous immigrant pockets in the cities specializing in their own cuisine. Miami has gained international recognition for its good **Cuban** food. *Platanitos* (plantain chips) and *tortilla de papa* (a Spanish omelette) are just two of the mouthwatering options. **Key lime pie** (which traditionally is yellow, not green, and served chilled, not frozen) is a must on many restaurant menus, each one claiming to make the best and most authentic one – try Sloppy Joe's in Key West.

---

**CITRUS FRUITS**

Polk County lies at the heart of the citrus belt thanks to its warm, sunny winters and hot summers. Lemon, lime and grapefruit are among the top crops but oranges are king, helping the state earn US$1.2 billion from its fruit annually. The first orange was thought to have been imported by the Spanish and now Florida exports a quarter of the world's orange crop. The only real threat to crops is the weather – an unexpected frost can destroy the year's harvest overnight.

**Stone crabs** are a south Florida delicacy, served with mayonnaise or 1000-island dressing. These particular crabs are strictly protected and may only be caught at certain times of the year once they have reached an acceptable size.

The variety of food is complemented by the variety of settings. Food courts or malls have become a fast-food alternative for those in a hurry or out shopping. You can sit at any table and buy meals from any of the surrounding food stalls, allowing your party to sample different menus in just one sitting.

Most cities have areas where many restaurants are concentrated – all you have to do is choose which gourmet delight to sample. Try Ybor City in Tampa, the Art Deco cafés of Miami or City Walk in Orlando.

Drinks complementing the meals are just as varied. American **beers** include Budweiser, Miller and Michelob, while Heineken leads the imports. You will be served iced water at every meal, though mineral water counts as an extra. Most soft drinks are available, except for tonic water – instead you'll be offered soda water, which is not as bitter. Be sure to try out the fresh **juices** – orange and grapefruit are musts – the main ingredient of many a cocktail, along with rum bought in from nearby Caribbean islands.

**Above:** *Seafood, fresh from the ocean, is on offer in the markets.*
**Below:** *This shop in John's Pass is paradise for anyone with a sweet tooth.*

# 2
# The Southeast

A hot city with a volatile Latin temperament, gleaming skyscrapers, clandestine wheeler-dealing and golden beaches packed with 'babes', is how many people picture **Miami**, capital of the Southeast.

But the *Miami Vice* image of the city is only partly accurate: it has far more to offer. The surrounding region presents a palm-dotted coastline with warm ocean waves, and the staggering **Everglades**. The Southeast is one of America's biggest playgrounds and visitors flock in their millions to frolic in the sun, swim in the lakes, dive among underwater corals, race yachts offshore, gamble, eat out, or simply sleep in.

Flying above **Miami International Airport** you can't fail to be impressed by the city's waterways. Cruise ships steam out of the harbour, powerboats lace the ocean with white spray and swift jet-skis roar between everything.

Despite being one of the last areas of the United States to be developed (the city only dates back a hundred years) Miami has become the region's focal point. Further up the coast millionaires in search of winter sun made their opulent homes in areas like **Palm Beach**, which exudes money with its polo grounds, manicured golf courses and glitzy boutiques.

Nearby **Fort Lauderdale** is a well-off, middle-class neighbourhood with a myriad channels and a bustling cruise port filled with yachts of every size. Travelling north you reach **Martin County** where state parks and towns like **Stuart**, which dates back to the 1880s, lend a nostalgic flavour of life gone by.

GEORGIA
Tallahassee

FLORIDA

GULF OF
MEXICO

Miami

---

### DON'T MISS

**\*\*\* South Beach, Miami:** one of the hottest places to see and be seen.
**\*\* Miami:** a downtown skyline made famous by many films, and just as spectacular in real life.
**\*\*\* Shopping:** some of the biggest malls in the world with great prices.
**\*\* Eating out:** both Miami and Fort Lauderdale pride themselves on their huge variety of venues.
**\*\*\* The Everglades:** natural wonderland threatened by encroaching development.

---

**Opposite:** *One of the first sights to greet tourists arriving in Miami by air.*

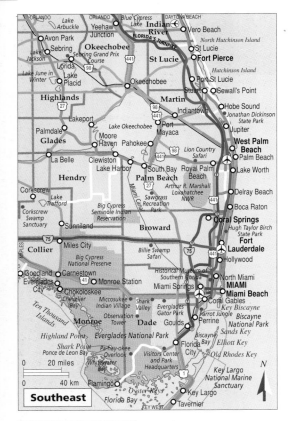

**Southeast**

## MIAMI

Miami and Miami Beach are actually two different cities, each with its own mood. Miami's mainland metropolis was little more than an overgrown village until the 1890s, when one local resident, **Julia Tuttle**, persuaded railroad king **Henry Flagler** to extend his tracks further south. By 1896 Miami was officially a city and by 1897 the first tourists arrived. But those early visionaries wanted Miami to be more than a mere **tourist resort** and so started to develop its port facilities. Today it is a major **crossroads** between United States, Caribbean and Latin America. Exploring the area as a whole is best done by car, but there are alternatives, particularly in the downtown region. Take a Metromover (individual motorized cars on a track) from **College/Bayside Station** and enjoy the skyline views. Two Metromover loops, both taking about 10 minutes, afford an excellent taste of the city atmosphere.

### Downtown **

The **Bayside Marketplace**, a short walk from the station across Biscayne Blvd, is a waterfront paradise with over 150 speciality shops, a large marina, food halls and street entertainers. It also offers frequent free music concerts, especially jazz and reggae. Just west of the station stands the 55-storey **Southeast Financial Center**, the tallest building in Florida. The Metromover takes you on to **Dade County Courthouse** (Government Center Station), once the tallest building south of Washington DC. Across the street is the **Metro–Dade Cultural Center**, a complex of water features and courtyards which houses three important buildings: the **Miami–Dade Main Library**, the

**Above:** *The Biltmore Hotel – a reminder of bygone glories.*

**Center for Fine Arts** and the **Historical Museum of Southern Florida**. The landmark **Gusman Center for the Performing Arts**, which offers numerous ballet and symphonic orchestra performances, can be found near First Street Station, on **Flagler Street**.

To explore the rest of Miami you need a car. **Coconut Grove**, first settled in 1884, was Miami's first real community. Today its emphasis is on the wealthy, and chic boutiques and elegant restaurants lie alongside tiny bars and street cafés. **CocoWalk** is at the heart, with retail and entertainment outlets in a European village-style setting. Be sure to visit the **Barnacle**, home of Miami pioneer Commodore Ralph Munroe, which contains much of its original furniture. **Charles Avenue**, the home of many Bahamian settlers who arrived in the late 1880s, retains its Victorian charm with red-brick sidewalks and ornate street lights. The pretty **Coconut Grove Playhouse** hosts Broadway plays each winter.

**Coral Gables**, the first planned community in the United States, was the brainchild of George Merrick. Its appeal has to do with the different 'village' designs, each representing the architectural style of a particular country or people, such as Chinese, Dutch–South African, French and Spanish. The **Biltmore Hotel**, a replica of the Giralda tower, is a classic Spanish example. Downtown Coral Gables also has its own shoppers' heaven, the **Miracle Mile**, lined with inviting shops and restaurants.

## LITTLE HAVANA

Little Havana, southwest of the downtown area, was the first stop for Cubans leaving their island after the Fidel Castro revolution, in the 1960s and 70s. Most of the original exiles have moved on, but there is still a Caribbean vibrancy to the area which is now home to a mix of Cubans, Nicaraguans and Colombians. The main street, Calle Ocho, is lined with coffee shops and fruit stalls. Try out specialities like plantain, rice and beans, chicken and pork, all cooked Cuban-style. The whole place comes alive each March for the week-long Little Havana festival, Carnaval Miami. On 17 April Cubans remember those who died in the failed Bay of Pigs invasion, with a ceremony on Cuban Memorial Boulevard.

### KEY BISCAYNE

Key Biscayne, a former coconut plantation, has remained relatively undeveloped, though affordable only to the very wealthy. It is accessible and worth a visit, as it offers one of the best beaches in Miami. **Crandon Park Beach** is rated among the top 10 in the country with its manicured grassy fringes and clean sand. **Virginia Key** to the north is site of the **Miami Seaquarium**, home of the TV star Flipper as well as Lolita, the killer whale.

## MIAMI BEACH

Miami Beach relishes its reputation as one of the hottest, hippest destinations in the United States. Singer Gloria Estefan and Island Records founder, Chris Blackwell, are among the celebrities who own hotels here. Aspirant models strive to be noticed at the top clubs and restaurants, many of which are owned by the likes of actor Sean Penn, and the popstar formerly known as Prince. You'll recognize so many settings that sometimes it may seem as as though you had wandered onto a film set by mistake.

### Art Deco District ★★★

Miami Beach, a collection of 17 islands in **Biscayne Bay**, was first developed by millionaire promoter Carl Graham Fisher in 1912 and has enjoyed 'boom or bust' prosperity since then. The famous **Art Deco District** along Ocean Drive was the product of a boom, enjoying a massive revival in the 1990s. At the **Art Deco Welcome Center** you can obtain details of the 800 protected buildings in the area and book walking or cycling tours.

**Ocean Drive** has proved a sublime film setting: pastel-hued buildings, vibrant blue skies, swaying palm trees and the ocean beyond create a perfect backdrop. **Collins Avenue** lies a block further and is another delight of grand architecture and fading glory. The Leslie, Impala, Carlyle and Cavalier are just some of the fine hotels.

On **Lincoln Road** in South Miami Beach is the

country's first pedestrian shopping mall, today enjoying a revival as an arts centre. The **Lincoln Road Colony Theater**, the **Miami City Ballet** (where you can watch rehearsals through the shop window) and the **South Florida Art Center** (which houses artists' studios and displays) should not be missed. At the southern tip of Miami Beach is **South Pointe Park** with views across the water to downtown Miami and east out to sea.

## The Islands **

Miami Beach is not just about SoBe, as South Beach is known. Check out **Watson Island**, which was created by dredging in 1931, and pay a visit to the celebrity-studded islands of **Palm**, **Star** and **Hibiscus**, whose residents have included Al Capone (who once lived at 93 Palm Avenue, Palm Island), film stars like Don Johnson at 8 Star Island, and Damon Runyan, whose address was 271 Hibiscus Island. Marvel at the **Morikami Museum** and **Japanese Garden** given to the city in 1961 by Kiyoshi Ichimura, the founder of Ricoh, where focal points are an octagonal pavilion, the Hakkaku-Do, and the eight-ton granite statue of *Hotei*, the smiling god of prosperity. There's also the **Flagler Memorial Monument** and the newly renovated **Bass Museum of Art**, which was designed by architect Arata Isozaki and houses a collection of paintings by the Old Masters.

**Above:** *Miami's Art Deco District has become a major tourist attraction.*
**Below:** *Miami Beach teems with visitors throughout the summer.*

You'll also want to spend time on the beach which stretches 10 miles (16km) down the coast. High-rise hotels line the beaches filled with sun-worshippers. Every available water sport can be tried out before eating or drinking in any of a countless choice of restaurants and bars.

**Above:** *An airboat glides through the Everglades.*

## THE EVERGLADES

Created by the waters of Lake Okeechobee draining slowly towards the sea after the summer rains, the Everglades fill almost all of south Florida between the coasts. With the water usually just a few inches deep and moving imperceptibly through sawgrass plains, the Everglades is aptly described as a 'river of grass'. Studding this low-lying landscape, however, are 'hummocks', tree islands where a slight rise in elevation enables trees to grow and provide a sanctuary for wildlife during the summer floods.

**Everglades National Park** spans 1.4 million acres (566,753ha) but consumes just 20 percent of the Everglades. Divided into three distinct visitor areas, the park is the best place to explore and comprehend the intricacies of the Everglades, although the area also has several state parks and other visitor-aimed areas, including those offering airboat rides which are popular but generally regarded as environmentally destructive and not permitted within the national park.

Each section of Everglades National Park can occupy a full-day, although an admission ticket is valid for use at any or all on the same day. The park is open all year but the mosquitoes and storms of summer make winter the prime time to visit. Flamingo is the closest section of the park to Miami, easily accessed off Highway 1. On the approach is the **Ernest Coe Visitor Center**, the largest of several park visitor centres and meriting a call even if you are not visiting this section of the park. From the centre, a 38-mile (98km) road continues into the park with clearly marked stop-points indicating rewarding short walking trails. Several of these pass through small forests of pine or palm, others such as the **Anhinga Trail**, are designed to bring views of wildlife. Another, **Pa-hay-okee Overlook**, reveals a vast expanse of sawgrass dotted by hammocks: the typical Everglades landscape. At the end of the route is dot-on-the-map **Flamingo**, established by hardy settlers in the 1890s. Here there are several short trails and guided walks and canoe trips, as well as the park's only (winter only) hotel. Further west, 35 miles (92km) from Miami off Highway-41, is **Shark Valley** where a two-hour narrated tram tour on a 15-mile (24.14km) loop road provides an excellent introduction to the Everglades, its seasonal cycles and its wildlife. On the route, an observation tower above a pond provides a good vantage point observing turtles, otters, a variety of birdlife and the ubiquitous alligators.

Much closer to Southwest Florida than Miami, **Ten Thousand Islands** is the best section of the park for boat or canoe exploration. Branching off Highway-41 forty miles from Shark Valley, Highway-29 passes first through the white-painted buildings of **Everglades City** before continuing to **Chokoloskee** where the land dissolves into a mangrove-fringed shoreline. From the small docks, boat tours voyage around the innumerable islands that define this section of the park, excellent for viewing birdlife and learning something of pioneer-era life.

The Miccosukee people have lived in the Everglades for many generations. On Highway 41 close to Shark Valley, the **Miccosukee Indian Village** displays handicrafts and cultural artefacts and mounts alligator wrestling shows. A less traditional venture is the Las Vegas-style Miccosukee

---

**ALLIGATORS**

The largest reptile in North America, the male *Alligator mississippiensis*, can grow up to 16ft (5m). The female is slightly smaller, measuring just under 8ft (2.4m). Alligators are cold-blooded creatures and need to lie in the sun to warm up enough to move. Once mobile they can develop surprising speed. As winter approaches, the rainy season ends and each alligator carves out a 'gator hole'. This hole, filled with underground water, conceals the lurking reptile as it lies in wait for thirsty prey such as deer, raccoons, otters and even birds.

**Below:** *The Everglade swamps are a perfect habitat for alligators.*

**Below:** *Rollerbladers and
joggers enjoy the promenade
in Fort Lauderdale.*
**Opposite:** *Fort Lauderdale's
Swimming Hall of Fame is a
monument to sunshine and
fine weather.*

hotel and casino (signposted off Highway-41 immediately
west of Miami), owned and run by the tribe, which
opened in 1999.

## FORT LAUDERDALE

The capital of Broward County was named after Major
William Lauderdale who established a fort here in 1838,
during the Seminole Indian wars. Until 1911 there were
just 175 residents and it was not until the boom years of
the 1920s that it became more than a dot on the map.

After 1960 this resort developed a huge following
among America's students who headed to the city in their
thousands for their traditional spring break. The riotous
success of these holidays put off many of the more sedate
tourists and eventually the city chiefs forced the students
on. Today it is considered one of the top family destinations with its 23 miles (37km) of beach and average
year-round temperature of 77°F (25°C).

### Downtown **

One way Fort Lauderdale shed its reputation for student
hedonism was by raising its cultural profile and developing the attractive **Riverwalk**, a river-side pathway lined
by sculpture and picnic stops that links much of historic
Fort Lauderdale with newer attractions such as the
**Museum of Discovery and Science** (tel: (954) 467 6637).
Here, interactive exhibits are certain to delight children
and also educate a few of their
parents into the ways of the natural world and beyond: not least
with a simulated trip to the
moon. Also in Downtown is the
1901 **Stranahan House**, providing revealing insights into the
lifestyles of frontier times, and
the **Museum of Art**, amongst the
diverse stock of which is the
US's premier collection works by
the influential 1950s European
CoBrA movement.

From Downtown, the palm-lined **Las Olas Boulevard** runs three miles (4.83km) to the coast lined by some of Fort Lauderdale's most upmarket shops and some of its most expensive homes. The latter occupy the waterside area known as **The Isles**, where the family car typically sits in the driveway while the family yacht is tethered at the rear. From Downtown, shuttle buses run the 12 miles to **Sawgrass Mills**, where 300 shops promising goods at less than normal retail prices make this one of the world's largest discount shopping malls.

## The Coast ★★

At its eastern end, Las Olas Boulevard expires directly opposite the Florida beach of a thousand postcards: golden sands fringed by blue ocean waters with palm trees offering vital shade from the sun. This idyllic scene stretches for several miles and accounts for the many small motels lining the side roads and the major hotels grouped at the southern end.

Aside from the glorious beach, coastal Fort Lauderdale also offers the **International Swimming Hall of Fame** (tel: (954) 462 6536), a short walk south of The Strip. This shrine to water sports is packed with medals and trophies of current and former champions, and oddities such as a stock of vintage swimming costumes and photos of a youthful Ronald Reagan during his time as a lifeguard.

Immediately north of the Strip, the **Hugh Taylor Birch State Park** occupies 180 bucolic acres (72.85ha) laced by walking trails beside a pine-fringed lagoon dotted with perfect picnic spots.

More tranquil gardens surround the nearby **Bonnet House**, a plantation-style abode built in the 1920s and open to visitors for worthwhile guided tours: tel: (954) 524 4736.

**Below:** *Whitehall was railroad magnate Henry Flagler's Palm Beach home.*
**Opposite:** *Polo is one of the favourite sports in upmarket Palm Beach.*

## PALM BEACH COUNTY

South of Palm Beach lies lovely **Boca Raton** which claims to be one of Florida's most attractive cities with its Spanish Revival style and 5 miles (8km) of glorious oceanfront. **Delray Beach**, a little further on, is worth a visit just for the Japanese Gardens and interesting Morikami Museum of Japanese Culture. The 200-acre (81ha) garden is famed for its bonsai which include the only known collection of Floridian bonsai plants. It also houses a Shinto shrine, a traditional Japanese teahouse and some picnic pavilions, as well as a recently added audiovisual exhibit about Japanese culture.

### Palm Beach ★★★

**Palm Beach** itself was created as an exclusive resort for the rich and famous and, more than a hundred years on, has retained its distinguished air. Less than 70 miles (112km) north of Miami, it is light years away in style and atmosphere. City centre bustle is replaced by elegant calm. Like so much of southern Florida, Palm Beach owes its success to railroad king **Henry Flagler**, since it was the first town that he developed on the east coast of Florida. He was helped by architect **Addison Mizner**, who had been commissioned by some of America's wealthiest – the Vanderbilts, the Whitneys and the Wanamakers – after an enormously successful debut with the Everglades Club on Worth Avenue.

**Whitehall**, Henry Flagler's magnificent and imposing home, still stands on Cocoanut Row in Palm Beach and is now open as a museum filled with many original furnishings and even a private railway car. Other attractions include an impressive art collection, complete with a masterful Gainsborough, as well as a 1200-pipe organ and unusual architecture – the

for beachside Fort
Lauderdale. The rate
includes free morning
coffee, a free newspaper
and free Cable TV service.

## Palm Beach
### LUXURY
**The Breakers**, One South
Country Road, Palm Beach,
tel: (561) 655-6611, fax:
(561) 659-8403. The ulti-
mate in glitz and glamour.

### MID-RANGE
**Heart of Palm**, 160 Royal
Palm Way, tel: (407) 655-
5600. Walking distance to
ocean. Value for money in
an otherwise expensive town.

**Palm Beach Historic Inn**,
365 S.County Road, Palm
Beach, FL33480, tel: (561)
832-4009, fax: (561) 832-
6255. Upmarket bed and
breakfast in a good location.

### BUDGET
**Days Inn**, 2300 45th Street,
West Palm Beach, tel: (800)
352-6786. Hotel chain offering basic facilities at low cost.

## Miami
**Blue Door at Delano**,
1685 Collins Ave, Miami
Beach, tel: (305) 674-6400.
French-Brazilian cuisine.
**Smith & Wollensky**, 1
Washington Ave, Miami
Beach, tel: (305) 673-2800,
American dining; reserva-
tions recommended.

**La Carreta**, 3632 SW Eighth
Street, tel: (305) 444-7501.
Cheap Cuban restaurant in
the heart of Little Havana.
**Lucky Cheng's**, 1412 Ocean
Drive, South Beach, tel: (305)
672-1505. Lively atmosphere.

## Fort Lauderdale
**Mai-Kai**, 3599 N Federal
Highway, tel: (954)
583-3272. Specializes in
Polynesian food.
**15th Street Fisheries**,
1900 SE 15th St, tel: (954)
763-2777. Old Florida style
seafood restaurant with a
$9 lunch, and pricier dinner
with everything from shrimp
to kangaroo and alligator.

## Palm Beach
**The Breakers**, 1 S County
Road, tel: (561) 655-6611.
Reservations required; dress
smartly for this famous hotel.

### TOURS AND EXCURSIONS
**Everglades Safari Park**,
26700 Tamiami Trl, Miami,
tel: (305) 226-6923, web:
www.evasafaripark.com
Guided airboat tours
through the glades.
**Sea Experience**, 801
Seabreeze Blvd, Fort
Lauderdale, tel (954)
467-6000, web: www.
seaexperience.com Snorkel
or ride in a glass-bottom
boat above coral reefs.
**Island Queen Sightseeing
Tours**, 401 Biscayne Rd,
Miami, tel: 0800-910-5119,
web: www.islandqueencruises.
com Take a ride along
Miami's coastline

### USEFUL CONTACTS
**Greater Miami Convention
& Visitors Bureau**, 701
Brickell Ave, tel: (305)
539-3000, web: www.
miamiandbeaches.com
**Greater Fort Lauderdale
Convention & Visitors
Bureau**, 1850 Eller Dr,
tel: (954) 765-4466,
web: www.sunny.org
**Palm Beach County
Convention & Visitors
Bureau**, 1555 Palm Beach
Lakes Blvd, tel: (561)
233-3000, web:
www.palmbeachfl.com
**Tropical Everglades
Visitor Association**,
160 US Hway 1, Homestead,
tel: 0800-388-9669, web:
www.tropicaleverglades.com

| MIAMI | J | F | M | A | M | J | J | A | S | O | N | D |
|---|---|---|---|---|---|---|---|---|---|---|---|---|
| AVERAGE TEMP. °F | 67 | 68 | 72 | 75 | 78 | 81 | 82 | 83 | 82 | 79 | 73 | 68 |
| AVERAGE TEMP. °C | 15 | 16 | 18 | 20 | 22 | 24 | 24 | 25 | 24 | 22 | 19 | 16 |
| HOURS OF SUN DAILY | 12 | 12 | 12 | 13 | 13 | 14 | 14 | 14 | 13 | 12 | 12 | 12 |
| RAINFALL in | 2 | 2 | 2 | 3 | 6.5 | 9 | 6 | 7 | 8 | 7 | 2.5 | 2 |
| RAINFALL mm | 51 | 51 | 51 | 76 | 165 | 229 | 152 | 179 | 203 | 179 | 63 | 51 |
| DAYS OF RAINFALL | 7 | 7 | 7 | 8 | 12 | 15 | 12 | 13 | 14 | 13 | 8 | 7 |

# 3
# Orlando and Central Florida

A dream come true for young and old alike, a dazzling fantasy land where everything is fun, where happy children play and carefree adults laugh – this is the home of **Mickey Mouse**, probably the most concentrated theme park area in the world. Whether you want to watch an alligator wrestling match, hug Minnie Mouse, eat out in the Wild West, or get your adrenaline pumping on daring rides, it is all possible here.

Take your pick from the delightful splendours of the **Magic Kingdom** and educational **Epcot**, the thrills of **Universal Studios** or **Wet 'n Wild** and **SeaWorld Orlando**. In an area where development really started only 100 years ago, the fun doesn't stop when the sun sets. Most theme parks are located in **Orlando** and on the road south towards **Kissimmee–St Cloud**. Many visitors fly straight to Orlando and then cherry-pick other attractions.

There are some choice **hotels** inside the Walt Disney World complex, where you can share your cornflakes with Mickey Mouse; or look for movie star magic at the Universal Studios properties. Alternatively you may prefer the cheaper option and stay slightly further away.

If you need to dilute the intensity of the parks, there are several tempting options. Why not explore the elegant shops of Orlando's **Winter Park**, or nearby Kissimmee–St Cloud which retains its cowboy style of old and hosts the **Silver Spurs Rodeo** in February each year. Admire the thoroughbred racehorses of **Ocala** or frolic in the shimmering lakes of **Lake County**. And to the south lies scenic **Polk County**, fragrant heart of the citrus belt.

**DON'T MISS**

\*\*\* **Magic Kingdom:** this is the reason most people visit Florida – the home of Mickey Mouse.
\*\*\* **Universal Studios:** classic films come to life with special effect rides.
\*\*\* **CityWalk:** the place to find restaurants, bars and evening entertainment
\*\* **Sea World:** with white knuckle rides and close encounters with creatures of the deep.
\*\* **Wet 'n Wild:** the very best way to cool off from the Florida heat.

**Opposite:** *Lazy River, Wet 'n Wild, is one of Orlando's less hair-raising attractions.*

**Central Florida**

## ORLANDO

The city of Orlando, now some 120 years old, was little more than a military outpost until 1875.

It is believed to have been named after **Orlando Reeves**, a soldier who was killed by an Indian arrow while on duty back in 1835. Agriculture dominated the early development, due to a year-round sunny, warm climate and the area's central position in the state. Almost 50 years ago, corporations began to arrive and the city started to blossom into the thriving metropolis it is today.

The reason that brings most people to this area is the winning combination of Mickey Mouse and Universal Studios in an area liberally dotted with theme parks and attractions. **Orlando International Airport** receives numerous direct scheduled flights from Europe, while Orlando Sanford Airport receives the international charter traffic.

It comes almost as a shock to find that Disney does not own the entire territory, so formidable has the image of the little mouse become, but theme parks aside, the downtown area offers an abundance of other interesting diversions. Sports fans, too, are well catered for. **Golfers** will be delighted to find over 130 golf courses within 45 minutes of the city (more than 100 courses within the Greater Orlando area). Course designers include Joe Lee, Tom Fazio and Robert Trent Jones. Others like Nick Price, Payne Stewart, Gary Player and Arnold Palmer all have homes in the city, which hosts at least four major tournaments a year. More than 800 **tennis courts** are available and spectators can choose between basketball's Orlando Magics, American football's Orlando Predators and ice hockey's Oralo Solar Bears.

### Charles Hosmer Morse Museum of American Art *

This museum in Winter Park is home to the world's most comprehensive collection of works by Louis Comfort Tiffany, including many of his most recognised windows, lamps and vases as well as jewellery, paintings and furniture.

**Above:** *Park Avenue in Winter Park is lined with glitzy boutiques and chic pavement cafés.*

### Mennello Museum of American Folk Art *

Florida's only museum dedicated to exhibiting the works of self-taught artists, including renowned folk artist Earl Cunningham.

### Albin Polasek Museum & Sculpture Gardens *

Listed on the National Register of Historic Places, this museum showcases nearly 200 of Czech-American sculptor Albin Polasek's sculptures and paintings.

### Zora Neale Hurston National Museum of Fine Arts *

Named for the renowned African-American writer, folklorist and anthropologist, this museum celebrates works by African artists. Hurston is also commemorated through an annual arts and humanities festival held in her hometown of Eatonville, just north of downtown Orlando.

### Orlando Museum of Art **

This museum at 2416 North Mills Avenue, Loch Haven Park, has a permanent collection of 19th- and 20th-century works, Mayan artefacts and a delightful 'Art Encounter', aimed at children. Its permanent *Art of the Ancient Americas Collection* includes more than 750 pieces of

> **WINDING DOWN**
>
> After a few hard days in the parks, Orlando has a variety of spa resorts for the ultimate pampering. **Wyndham Palace Resort & Spa** and **The Greenhouse Spa** at the Portofino Bay Hotel are inside the Disney and Universal parks respectively while the newest and largest is the **Ritz-Carlton Spa**, Grand Lakes Orlando. Two more are due to open in autumn 2004, the **Regent Winter Park** and the **Omni Orlando Resort** at ChampionsGate.

ancient art from 30 different cultural groups in North, Central and South America. It is considered to be the broadest and most representative collection in the Southeast United States.

## WALT DISNEY WORLD RESORT

Walt Disney World Resort is a massive complex of theme parks and housing four theme parks, two water parks, 27 resort hotels (17 owned and operated by Walt Disney World), 99 holes of golf on six courses, two full-service spas, Disney's wedding pavilion, Disney's Wide World of Sports complex and Downtown Disney, an entertainment, shopping and dining complex.

### The Magic Kingdom ★★★

For many people this park epitomizes Walt Disney World and, with more than 40 major rides and shows spread across a 107-acre site, is the first stop on any visit. Call tel: (407) 824-4321 for opening times. Enchanting **Cinderella Castle** lies at the heart of the Magic Kingdom, its seven themed lands radiating outward like the spokes of a wheel. **Main Street USA**, lined with old-time shops and restaurants, leads you from the main entrance to the castle and is the site of the daily **Parade** at 15:00.

**Adventureland** is home to the quaint **Swiss Family Treehouse**, the sweet tunes of the **Enchanted Tiki Birds**, a steamy **Jungle Cruise** and the **Extraterrorestial Alien Encounter**. The pace picks up a bit in **Frontierland** where you will encounter the first white-knuckle ride – the world's longest flume drop from **Splash Mountain** – as well as the slightly tamer **Big Thunder Mountain Railroad** and **Tom Sawyer Island**. **Liberty Square** takes a look back at America's history. Take a steamboat ride and visit the interesting **Hall of Pres-**

**Below:** *Epcot's high-tech wizardry impresses young and old alike.*

© DISNEY ENTERPRISES, INC.

idents and the spooky **Haunted Mansion** filled with cobwebs, apparitions and creepy sounds.

**Fantasyland** is perfect for little visitors, offering Peter Pan, Dumbo, Mad Hatter's Tea Party and Snow White rides and carousels, and the singing dolls of **It's a Small World**.

**Mickey's Toontown Fair** is where you'll find Mickey and his friends in a cartoon world brought to life. Stroll along the **Walk of Fame**, where characters' voices are activated by stepping on the stars.

Older visitors will not want to skip **Tomorrowland** and its highlight ride, **Space Mountain**, an unnerving roller coaster in the dark. Nervous visitors may prefer the calmer **Grand Prix Raceway**, which is really aimed for children.

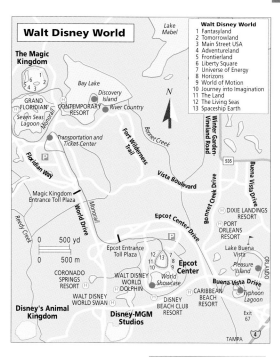

Walt Disney World

1 Fantasyland
2 Tomorrowland
3 Main Street USA
4 Adventureland
5 Frontierland
6 Liberty Square
7 Universe of Energy
8 Horizons
9 World of Motion
10 Journey into Imagination
11 The Land
12 The Living Seas
13 Spaceship Earth

## Epcot ★★★

Covering 260 acres and split into two areas, Epcot is divided between **Future World** focusing on discovery and scientific achievements and **World Showcase** reflecting the cultures of the world. Mission Space and Test Track are among the latest attractions, along with the Tower of Terror.

## Disney-MGM Studios ★★

A working film, TV, radio and animation studio that was home to the making of *Lilo and Stitch* as well as a theme park featuring more than 20 rides, attractions and shows.

**Right:** *Universal Studios offers rides, stunt shows and movie memorabilia.*
**Opposite:** *Killer whales perform daily at SeaWorld Orlando.*

---

### DISCOVERY COVE

Adjacent to SeaWorld Orlando is Discovery Cove, where visitors can snorkel through coral reefs with thousands of marine animals and swim among **dolphins**. Reservations are required, tel: 877 4DIS-COVERY. Or see the website: www.discoverycove.com

---

### GOLFING FACTS

• 123 courses lie within a 45-minute drive of downtown Orlando.
• Nick Price, Lee Janzen, Payne Stewart, Ian Baker-Finch, Gary Player, Corey Pavin and Arnold Palmer are among the golfing stars to own a home here.
• Arnold Palmer, Jack Nicklaus, Tom Fazio and Robert Trent Jones have all designed courses in the area.
• Walt Disney World Resort has six courses alone within the complex.
• The World Cup of Golf was hosted by Lake Nona in 1993 and Grand Cypress in 1991.
• PGA tour events include the Walt Disney World–Oldsmobile Classic and the Bay Hill Invitational. LPGA events include the Chrysler Tournament of Champions and the HealthSouth Classic.

---

## AROUND DISNEY
### Universal Studios ★★★

No visit would be complete without experiencing the fabulous shows, rides and thrills of Universal Studios, although this venue appeals mainly to older children and adults. The Studios, located at 1000 Universal Studios Plaza, are open from 09:00 daily.

**Terminator 2: Battle Across Time** is billed as the world's first 4D, interactive attraction. Also do not miss **Earthquake**, **Jaws**, **Back to the Future**, **Twister**, **Shrek 4D**, or **The Revenge of the Mummy**, all of which are guaranteed to cause sweaty palms, shrieks and palpitations.

Adjacent to Universal Studios is Universal's second park, **Islands Of Adventure**. This excellent park features two of the world's best roller-coaster rides, **Duelling Dragons** and the **Incredible Hulk Coaster**, as well as the 3D ride – **Amazing Adventure of Spiderman**. Two new rides have been added on Marvel Super Hero Island – **The Flying Unicorn** and **Storm Force**. Adjacent to the park is **CityWalk**, with themed restaurants and nightlife venues.

### Wet 'n Wild Orlando ★★

This theme park at 6200 International Drive recently added a white-knuckle toboggan ride to its long list of attractions. If you want to get your adrenaline pumping, then don't miss this heart-stopping, six-storey drop down a tunnel.

The area includes water slides, flumes, lazy rivers and pools to keep water babies of all ages happy for hours. Open year round, though times vary according to season.

### Ripley's Believe It or Not! Museum *

A peculiar attraction not to be missed, this rather bizarre museum, also on International Drive, is housed in a strange building made to look as though it is about to collapse and provides odd entertainment for relatively low cost. Open 09:00–24:00 daily.

### SeaWorld Orlando **

Established in 1973, SeaWorld Orlando, on 7007 SeaWorld Drive, offers the stunning **Wild Arctic**, which combines a flight over the frozen North and close-up encounters with wildlife including polar bears. Other attractions are the **Shamu Stadium**, **Pacific Point Reserve**, **Terrors of the Deep** and **Kraken**, billed as the highest and fastest roller-coaster in Orlando. Open 09:00–19:00 in winter, 09:00–20:00 in spring and autumn, 09:00–23:00 in summer.

### Discovery Cove ***

Adjacent to SeaWorld Orlando is Discovery Cove, where visitors can snorkel through coral reefs with marine animals and swim among dolphins. Reservations are required, tel: 877 4DISCOVERY. Or visit the website: www.discoverycove.com

### Nightlife Attractions *

Evening entertainment is as varied as the theme parks. Venues are highly competitive and forever trying to outdo one another. They also extend the fantasy flavour of Orlando, from **Makahiki Luau** at SeaWorld Orlando, where guests are whisked off to Hawaii, to the **Sleuths Mystery Dinner Show** at 7508 Republic Drive, with its six-nightly who-dunnit mysteries. Or enjoy country music courtesy of **Dolly Parton's Dixie Stampede Dinner & Show** at 8251 Vineland Ave.

---

**SHOPPING**

Shopaholics beware – retail space abounds in Orlando:
• Altamonte Mall, Osceola Square, Orlando Fashion Square, Seminole Town Center.
• Belz Factory Outlet World: more than 160 discount stores.
• Orlando's Antique Row.
• Park Avenue: upmarket boutiques in Winter Park.
• Theme parks: wide variety of merchandise for sale.
• Downtown Disney and CityWalk.
• Airport: last-minute souvenirs.

**OUT IN THE WILDS**

Even the most ardent theme park fan will soon become aware that beyond the domain of Mickey Mouse Florida has many expanses of undeveloped and often untamed land. Be it swamp, forest or prairie, sizeable chunks of the state are variously protected as federally-run national parks, such as Everglades and Biscayne, or Florida-run state parks. Many lesser known areas also enjoy various levels of protection, such as the Lower Suwannee National Wildlife Refuge near Cedar Key and the Timucuan Ecological and Historical Reserve near Jacksonville.

## AROUND ORLANDO

Leaving the glittering illusions of Orlando behind, you discover that central Florida has some unspoilt areas that look much the same now as they must have when discovered by the Europeans a few hundred years ago.

To the east, near the town of Christmas, lies the **Tosohatchee State Reserve**, said to be one of the most pristine sites in the region. Visitors are free to roam through the park, along 40 miles (65km) of the **Florida Trail**. During hunting season you are obliged to wear bright orange warning vests, and it's best to call ahead to warn the park rangers of your arrival. Also to the east of Orlando is an artificial wetland area – the **Orlando Wilderness Park**. This is an excellent place for bird spotting, but is closed during the hunting season which lasts from 1 October to 20 January.

Heading north from Orlando, you pass through **Maitland**. Visit the popular **Art Center**, which promotes American art and artists in an attractive rural setting. Victoriana rules supreme at the **Historic Waterhouse Residence and Carpentry Shop Museums**, which were built in 1884 and maintain their stately Victorian air to this day. Equally interesting are the **Maitland Historical Museum** and the **Telephone Museum**.

Nostalgia is the key note at **Sanford** where the steamboat, *Grand Romance*, puffs along the St Johns River with up to 350 dinner guests on board.

**Below:** *Glass-bottom boats travel across Silver Springs in search of alligators, fish and turtles.*

### Lake County *

Further to the northwest of Orlando, the St Johns River is joined by the Wekiwa River at Apopka, which is the home of the **Wekiwa Springs State Park**. The numerous tributaries feeding into the river form perfect canoeing trails, while energetic hikers can choose from several splendid, well-mapped paths.

Beyond, and pretty as a postcard, the tiny village of **Mount Dora** perches on top of a bluff overlooking Lake Dora. Many of the quaint cottages decorated with flower-filled window boxes are now art galleries and tempting antique shops, reminiscent of New England rather than Florida. **Renninger's Twin Markets**, held here each weekend, attract up to 500 antique dealers.

**Lake Dora** lies in the heart of Lake County, which was named for its abundance of water. A canal, said to be one of the most beautiful in the world, connects lakes Dora and Eustis and is perfect for relaxing cruises.

Further north, in Marion County, the landscape changes from the typical Florida flatlands to rolling green hills. This lush farmland is filled with cattle and thoroughbred race horses. Some of the 400 horse farms have open days, when visitors can visit the facilities and watch training sessions.

### Ocala **

Near Ocala be sure to visit the **Ocala National Forest** with its sand pine trees and **Silver Springs**, one of the state's oldest attractions and the world's largest natural spring. The Springs contain alligators, turtles and large-mouth bass. Travel on a glass-bottom boat – the water is so clear here that one can see to a depth of 80ft (24m).

**Above:** *Marion County is home to some of Florida's top horse breeders.*

---

**FISHING**

Lake County is named after its 1440 lakes. Many people visit the area in search of peace and quiet after the frenzy of Orlando. Fishing is a popular pastime here, the waters containing some 115 species. The largemouth bass is Florida's official fresh-water fish. If you are over 16 years of age you may need a fishing or hunting licence in some parts of the state. For details of local regulations contact the **Florida Game and Fresh Water Fish Commission**, tel: (904) 488-1960 or 488-2975.

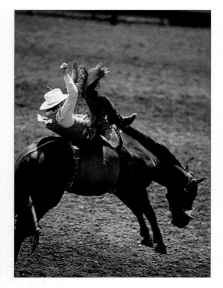

**ANNUAL EVENTS
AROUND ORLANDO**

**January** • Florida Citrus Festival and Polk County Fair.
**February** • Silver Spurs Rodeo, held in Kissimmee since 1944.
**March** • Four-day Kissimmee Bluegrass Music Festival.
**April** • Polk City week of aviation events.
**May** • Annual outdoor Art Festival at Lakeland.
**June** • Bi-annual International Orchid Fair, last held 1996.
**October** • Florida Horse and Agricultural Festival, Ocala.
**November** • Chrysanthemum Festival, Cypress Gardens.
**December** • Florida Citrus Sailfest at Lake Monroe.
**Mid-December** • Very Merry Christmas Parade, the Magic Kingdom, Walt Disney World.

Or take an exciting jeep safari or jungle cruise. Children will enjoy the **Wild Waters** next to the park, with its giant wave pool, slides and water cannons. For opening times call tel: (904) 236-2121 or 800 274-7458.

The 350-acre (142ha) **Ocala National Forest** incorporates more than 100 miles (160km) of horse trails and 65 miles (105km) of the Florida National Scenic Trail. One of the most enjoyable ways to experience the park is by leisurely canoe or on horseback. There are also dive and snorkel sites.

Among Ocala's attractions is **The Appleton Museum of Art** with its regularly changing exhibitions of antiquities dating back 5000 years. Here you can marvel at early Rembrandt etchings, a 'Thinker' by Rodin (cast from the *original* mould), Turkish prayer rugs, a wooden Tibetan saddle and Japanese figurines. Open 10:00–16:30 Tuesday–Saturday, 13:00–17:00 Sunday.

The distinctly 20th-century **Don Garlits Museum of Drag Racing** houses a collection of antique cars, as well as the famous 'swamp rats' (specialized drag racing vehicles). Open 09:00–17:30 daily, except Christmas Day.

## Clermont *

Clermont, to the west of Orlando, is home to the fascinating **House of Presidents Wax Museum**. Figures range from George Washington to Bill Clinton. It is also at the centre of Florida's wine production, and vineyards carpet the landscape. With the help and advice of the nearby University of Florida, the region now produces very palatable wines. **Lakeridge Winery and Vineyards** is open to the public for wine-tasting and tours. The other main crop around Clermont is citrus fruit and from the **Florida Citrus Tower** on Highway 27 you can enjoy a stunning panoramic view across the region.

## Kissimmee ★★

Within easy driving of Orlando, the Kissimmee–St Cloud area offers plenty of themed entertainment, some as bizarre as the **Tupperware World Headquarters** (not open to public), while managing to retain old world charm. The emphasis here is on cowboys, rodeos and the outdoors rather than Mickey Mouse, but the hotels are happy to sell themselves as the perfect spot from which to explore Walt Disney World, just a few miles north.

Kissimmee is slightly closer to Walt Disney World, lying on the northwestern tip of **Lake Tohopekaliga**, while St Cloud lies just a few kilometres to the east on the southern shores of **East Lake Tohopekaliga**.

As you head south from Orlando along S Orange Blossom Trail, **Gatorland** is worth a stop to shiver at the sight of more than 5000 prehistoric-looking alligators. The park has thrilling daily shows such as Gator Jumparoo, Gator Wrestling and Snakes Alive, and a restaurant where gator ribs are on the menu. Open 08:00–dusk. Friendlier animals are found at the **Green Meadows Petting Farm**, which provides a two-hour tour of 300 farm animals, with younger visitors being encouraged to touch. Open 09:30–16:00 daily; the park closes at 17:30.

Another escape from the brash commercialism found along Highway 192, Kissimmee's main thoroughfare, is provided by **Celebration**. This much publicised Disney-planned residential community is intended to recapture the spirit of small-town America.

### HORSE RACING

Ocala gained acclaim as a centre for horse racing when a locally bred horse called Needles was the surprise winner of the **Kentucky Derby**. Today there are some 400 horse farms in the area, many of which welcome visitors. To see the farms and enjoy the rolling hills and green countryside, drive southwest out of Ocala and down Route 200 towards Holder. The largest racecourse in Florida is the **Gulfstream Park** track between Miami and Fort Lauderdale where the US$500,000 **Florida Derby** is run each March.

**Opposite:** *Kissimmee is cowboy country, and rodeos are held regularly.*
**Left:** *The safest way to see alligators is at Gatorland south of Orlando.*

Those with a head for heights and speed can become United States fighter pilots for the day with F-16 trained pilots on hand to teach aerial combat manoeuvres. **Fighter Pilots USA** is based at the town's small airport. Slightly closer to the ground is the **Flying Tigers Warbird Air Museum** on 231 Hoagland Boulevard with its World War II aircraft and flying shows. You can also book a flight for a bird's-eye view of the Orlando area.

Kissimmee–St Cloud has its own water park, **Water Mania**. This 38-acre (15ha) park has all the usual thrills and spills with slides and wave pools as well as Wipe Out, a simulated surf ride.

The **World of Orchids** at 2501 Old Lake Wilson Road houses the first permanent indoor display of orchids in the world, in a conservatory measuring 29,000ft$^2$ (2700m$^2$). Recreating the steamy heat of the tropics, the park holds thousands of orchids in a variety of settings, hosts three orchid fairs a year and exports its product worldwide.

The attractive Old Town shopping centre contains inviting, old-fashioned shops and restaurants, as well as a giant Ferris wheel and museums.

**Golfing** is a major attraction and many big-name designers have courses here – as well as some of the celebrity golfers including Greg Norman, Tom Watson, Arnold Palmer, Johnny Miller, Jack Nicklaus and Gary Koch. The **Reunion Resort & Club** has two of the newest courses – the 6343m (6937yd) Legacy course and the 6636m (7257yd) Independence course, designed by Arnold Palmer and Tom Watson respectively.

**Below:** *The dinner show at Arabian Nights offers Eastern delights such as belly dancing.*

As in Orlando, most of the evening entertainment venues and restaurants here have climbed on the fantasy bandwagon. **Arabian Nights** (*see* At a Glance p. 61) brings exotic legends to life. At **Medieval Times**, visitors get to see knights, maidens, nobles, sword fights and jousting tournaments while feasting on hearty medieval fare. There is also a museum which offers a trip through a dungeon and shows by craftsmen in traditional costumes. **Wild Bill's Wild West Dinner Show** has a local flavour: cowboy antics, native Comanche Indian dancing and square dancing adding a touch of the Ol' West.

**Above:** *While watching the show at Medieval Times, enjoy a wholesome meal – using only your hands.*

## Polk County **

Like Lake County further north, Polk County, to the south, is a superb inland retreat, offering nature lovers over 600 **freshwater lakes**. Lining these tranquil lakes are the big, fragrant **citrus groves** and deep, dark **pine forests** that have helped to make the area a major scenic attraction.

This county, however, offers a pleasant mix of natural as well as cultural offerings. The **Black Hills Passion Play**, which depicts the last seven days of Christ's life, is held around Easter at the **Lake Wales Amphitheatre**. The big **Polk Museum of Art** is one of the largest museums in central Florida and the **Mulberry Phosphate Museum** houses some interesting displays of petrified dinosaur bones excavated in the surrounding region.

Among the places to visit is **Bok Tower Gardens**. This 128-acre (52ha) expanse provides a sanctuary for both fauna and flora. In the middle of the garden a 57-bell carillon tower chimes the hours, while musicians wander around and a varied programme of year-round concerts is sure to delight music lovers. The gardens were closed temporarily after Hurricane Charley (the second most expensive hurricane ever to hit the region) hit in August 2004 but were undergoing repairs to reopen during the winter of 2004/05.

The **Fantasy of Flight** is an aviation-themed attraction that takes visitors back to early flight, World War I, World War II and beyond. Tour one of the largest private collections of aircraft in the world, experience a simulated battle mission over the South Pacific or cruise over central Florida in a hot air balloon.

### LAKE TOHOPEKALIGA

Seminole Indians once lived on the shores of this lake which today separates St Cloud and Kissimmee. The lake is also the setting for special events like the annual Spring Bluegrass Festival, and the autumn Boating Jamboree.

# Orlando and Central Florida at a Glance

## BEST TIMES TO VISIT

The **summer** months, from June to October, are **hot** and humid with frequent short **thunderstorms**, but crowds are reduced. The peak **winter** months are **December** to **February**, when Americans abandon the cold northeast and head for the winter sun. Parks are packed, but the weather is mild and drier, and so better for queuing.

## GETTING THERE

**Orlando International Airport** receives scheduled air traffic while **Orlando Sanford** receives the international charter flights. Many European carriers fly direct; United States airlines has good domestic connections. Most hotels offer free **shuttles** from and to the airport. Public **buses** service the downtown area; there are also limousine and taxi services, both fairly expensive. Orlando and Kissimmee are on the **Florida Turnpike**, a toll-road from Miami and on **Interstate 4** which crosses the state from Tampa to Daytona Beach. Both 1–4 and **US192** pass the main access roads for Walt Disney World. US 192 takes you near the main entrance of the Magic Kingdom. **Amtrak** offers train services to Winter Park, and to Kissimmee.

## GETTING AROUND

**Driving** around Orlando is quite straightforward and 1–4 is the main artery. Plenty of **taxis** are available and a number of the attractions offer **shuttle** services from hotels. On International Drive, **I-Ride** shuttle buses operate a 15-minute service, running from 07:00–24:00. Children ride free of charge.

## WHERE TO STAY

### Orlando
#### LUXURY
**Marriott's Orlando World Center**, 8701 World Center Drive, tel: (407) 239-4200, fax: 621-0638. Massive hotel with many facilities; attracts many convention delegates.

#### MID-RANGE
**Clarion Plaza**, 9700 International Drive, tel: (407) 352-9700. Next to the Convention Center, 1.2 miles (2km) from Sea World.
**Las Palmas Hotel**, 6233 International Drive, tel: (407) 351-3900, fax: 352-5597. About 14 miles (20km) from downtown area, but close to the major attractions.

#### BUDGET
**Quality Inn Plaza**, 3330 W Colonial Drive, tel: (407) 299-6710, fax: 296-4005. Over 1000 rooms, conveniently located.

### Disney
#### LUXURY
**Grand Floridian**, Lake Buena Vista, tel: (407) 824-3000, fax: 354-1866. A grand hotel at a grand price; very convenient for Disney with a monorail stop outside.

#### MID-RANGE
**Walt Disney World Dolphin**, 1500 Epcot Resort Boulevard, tel: (407) 934-4000. Inside the Walt Disney complex. Massive Disney-style hotel.

#### BUDGET
**Disney's Pop Century Resort**, tel: (407) 938-4000, fax: (407) 938-4040. Part of Disney's wide world of sports complex and near to the animal kingdom.

### Kissimmee
#### MID-RANGE
**Quality Inn Maingate West**, 7785 W Highway–192, tel: (407) 396-1828, fax: 396-1305. Suitable for families; children's restaurant, pool and regular shuttles to Disney.

## WHERE TO EAT

Orlando and Kissimmee have turned dinner theatres into a lucrative art form.

### Orlando
**Ran-Getsu of Tokyo**, 8400 International Drive, tel: (407) 345-0044. Japanese dining – reservations recommended, dinner only.
**Hard Rock Café Orlando**, City Walk, Universal Studios Orlando, tel: (407) 892-7311. Guitar-shaped building with more than 500 items of rock 'n roll memorabilia to admire while eating.

## Orlando and Central Florida at a Glance

**Christini's**, 7600 Dr Phillips Blvd, tel: (407) 345-8770. Upmarket northern Italian cuisine; book ahead.

### Disney World
Restaurant information and reservations tel: (407) 939-3463.

**Magic Kingdom**
King Stefan's Banquet Hall. Prime rib, seafood and other meals fit for a king.

**Liberty Square**
The Liberty Tree Tavern. Recreation of a colonial inn; wholesome American food.

**Epcot**
The World Showcase. 12 restaurants with menus from around the world.

### Kissimmee
**Arabian Nights**, 6225 W Irlo Bronson Memorial Highway, tel: (407) 239-9223. Dinner show offering Eastern delights such as belly dancing.

**Medieval Times Dinner and Tournament**, 4510 W Irlo Bronson Memorial Highway, tel: (407) 396-1518. Toast King Henry during a four-course dinner with unlimited beer, wine and soft drinks.

**Pirate's Dinner Adventure**, 6400 Carrier Drive, tel: (407) 248-0590.

**Dolly Parton's Dixie Stampede Dinner & Show**, 8251 Vineland Ave, Orlando, tel: (407) 238-4455. Horses, buffalo, singing and dancing.

SHOPPING

**Orlando Mount Dora Village Merchants**, Mount Dora, tel: (352) 735-1191, fax: 383-7524. Located in Central Florida, offering a look at a quaint town with antiques, boutiques and cuisine.

**The Florida Mall**, 8001 S. Orange Blossom Tr, Orlando, tel: (407) 851-6255, fax: 855-1827. Unparalleled shopping in Central Florida – fabulous fashions, exceptional eateries and delightful diversions. Features Burdines, Dillard's, JC Penney, Parisian, Saks Fifth Avenue, Sears, and more than 250 specialty shops.

**The Mall at Millenia**, 4200 Conroy Road, Orlando, tel: (407) 363-3555. Good shopping and restaurants.

### TOURS AND EXCURSIONS

**Bill's Airboat Adventure**, tel: (407) 977-3214, guided boat tours on the St John's River on board six-person airboats.

**Orange Blossom Balloons**, tel (407) 239 7677, champagne balloon flights at sunrise, reservationa required.

**Walt Disney World, Sea-World** and **Universal Studios Orlando** offer **guided tours**. Enquire at entrance.

### USEFUL CONTACTS

**Central Florida Convention and Visitors Bureau**, 1339 Helena Rd, Winter Haven, tel: (863) 298-7565, web: www.sunsational.org

**Orlando Official Visitor Centre**, 8723 International Drive, Suite 101, Orlando, tel: (407) 363-5872, web: www.orlandoinfo.com

**Kissimmee/St Cloud Convention and Visitors Bureau**, 1925 E Irlo Bronson Memorial Highway, Kissimmee, FL34744, tel: (407) 847-5000, web: www.floridakiss.com

**Lake County Convention & Visitors Bureau**, 20763, US Highway 27, Groveland, FL34736, tel: (904) 429-3673, web: www.lakecountryfl.com

**Walt Disney World Central Reservation Office** (for in-park accommodation), Suite 300, Lake Buena Vista, 32830, tel: (407) 934-7639.

**Walt Disney World Information**, Box 10040, Lake Buena Vista, FL32830, tel: (407) 824-4321, www.disneyworld.com

**Universal Orlando**, 1000 Universal Studios Plaza, Orlando, tel: (407) 363-8000, www.universalorlando.com

| ORLANDO | J | F | M | A | M | J | J | A | S | O | N | D |
|---|---|---|---|---|---|---|---|---|---|---|---|---|
| AVERAGE TEMP. °F | 49 | 54 | 56 | 63 | 67 | 75 | 75 | 74 | 74 | 67 | 58 | 52 |
| AVERAGE TEMP. °C | 8 | 9 | 13 | 17 | 19 | 23 | 23 | 23 | 23 | 19 | 14 | 11 |
| HOURS OF SUN DAILY | 12 | 12 | 12 | 13 | 13 | 14 | 14 | 14 | 13 | 12 | 12 | 12 |
| RAINFALL in | 2 | 3 | 3 | 2 | 4 | 7 | 8 | 6 | 6 | 3 | 2 | 2 |
| RAINFALL mm | 53 | 71 | 81 | 55 | 100 | 187 | 197 | 160 | 142 | 71 | 45 | 46 |
| DAYS OF RAINFALL | 7 | 8 | 8 | 7 | 9 | 13 | 14 | 12 | 11 | 9 | 7 | 7 |

# 4
# The East Coast

Speed is what this part of Florida is known for, from the deafening roar of rockets blasting into space to the burst of motor-sports action at the world-famous **Daytona International Speedway**. The region is also home to an extraordinary mix of beaches, parks, waterways and preserves that offer families plenty to see and do.

Halfway along lies the **Space Coast**, where the high technology of **Cape Canaveral** and **Titusville's Space Camp**, not to mention the **Astronaut Hall of Fame** (part of the Kennedy Space Center), rival for your attention. **Shuttle launches** take place throughout the year and should not be missed. The explosive blast-off of rocket engines contrasts strongly with the tranquillity of the nearby **National Wildlife Refuge** at Merritt Island and the parks surrounding DeLand.

The **Daytona Beach** area is well-known for its fabled 23-mile stretch of beaches. It is on the area's expansive shoreline that **Sir Malcolm Campbell** took Land Speed Records to a new dimension with his earth-shattering drive of 276mph (442kph) back in 1935. Modern speed addicts have to travel out west to the deserts of Nevada to find enough space to beat his times. Visitors can view Campbell's record-setting automobile the *Bluebird V*, along with a short film detailing his record attempts on the area's beaches, at DAYTONA USA – the official attraction of NASCAR.

Visitors to Florida's east coast should also take time to relax and enjoy the incredible natural beauty of long sandy beaches, dramatic Atlantic coastlines – and the lure

| DON'T MISS |
| --- |

**\*\*\* Kennedy Space Center:** history of space exploration, rockets and shuttle launches.
**\*\* Daytona Beach:** longtime vacation mecca for families and car-racing enthusiasts.
**\*\* Merritt Island National Wildlife Refuge:** miles of undisturbed sand dunes and excellent bird-watching.
**\*\* Cocoa Beach:** very good surfing and the best spots to watch shuttle launches.
**\* Main Street Pier**, **Daytona Beach:** fairground rides and shops on a traditional east coast boardwalk setting.

**Opposite:** *Rockets dwarf the visitors at Rocket Park, Kennedy Space Center.*

**Offshore breezes** and slightly **cooler** temperatures make this a popular tourist area. Summer highs reach 88°F (31°C) July–September. In winter the highs are 75°F (24°C), but can drop down to 50°F (10°C) between January and March.

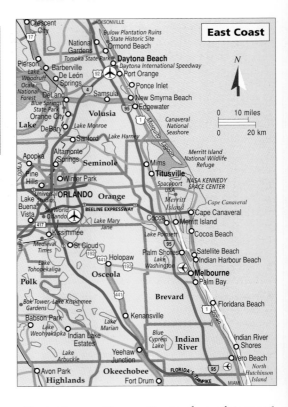

**East Coast**

### GOLFING

The east coast is famed for its excellent golf courses. **Vero Beach** has 14 courses around the city and, although some are private, most welcome visitors. The 28 courses situated around **Daytona Beach** include the Ladies' Professional Golfers' Association's Legends and Champions courses, chosen as the headquarters of the United States LPGA.

of buried treasure. **Treasure Coast** to the south is named after the spilled contents of countless ships that floundered on the sand bars well within sight of land. Experts claim that some 1800 Spanish galleons were wrecked on these shores more than 400 years ago and that their priceless cargo still remains, awaiting discovery.

Many golf courses and extensive water-sports facilities complete the picture of a superb outdoor area with plenty of distraction on offer for the entire family.

## VERO BEACH

At the centre of the Indian River citrus belt, the affluent resort of Vero Beach has a healthy mix of industries, but tourism is one of the faster growing. There are some 15 **golf courses** (not all are open to the public), numerous **boat charters** for fishing, canoeing and sailing and several well-maintained **tennis clubs**.

Museums in this city include the **Center for the Arts** on 3001 Riverside Park Drive, which mixes local, national and international exhibitions and is well known for its many seminars, concerts, work-

shops and festivals. The **McLarty Museum** situated on 13180 N Route, open 10:00–16:30 daily, concentrates mainly on Indian artefacts and recovered treasure and is dedicated to the hurricane of 1715 in which an entire fleet of treasure-laden Spanish galleons perished. The **Mel Fisher Treasure Museum**, at 1322 US1 in neighbouring Sebastian also houses artefacts salvaged from the numerous ships that floundered on this coast. The **Indian River Citrus Museum** takes a look at the industry behind the wealth of the region, while the **Historical Society** has an

exhibition at the city railway station; both are located on 14th Avenue. **McKee Botanical Gardens**, on the east side of US1, was first opened in 1932 and its stock of plants is refurbished annually by the Indian River Land Trust.

The **Environmental Learning Center** on Live Oak Drive offers daytime and evening field trips through saltmarsh and mangrove swamp areas, to educate visitors about the surrounding habitat.

The camp site at **Sebastian Inlet State Recreation Area**, to the north of Vero Beach, is flanked by the Atlantic Ocean to the east and the Indian River to the west. Not only good for hiking and cycling, it also has snorkelling and scuba-diving opportunities – for certified divers only – and offers some of the best saltwater fishing on the east coast.

**Above:** *The citrus farming industry made Floridians wealthy at the turn of the century and still provides thousands of jobs.*
**Below:** *Golf has become big business – Florida has more golf courses than any other American state.*

## BEACHES

Avoid the crowds and head out to the shores of Ormond By-The-Sea, Ponce Inlet, Klondike, Floridana, Canaveral National Seashore and Sebastian Inlet State Recreation Park. Or you can go for fun in the sun with the crowds at Cocoa, Satellite, Indian Harbor and Melbourne beaches. The best surfing is possible at Ponce Inlet, New Smyrna Beach, Cocoa and Playa-linda beaches or Sebastian Inlet.

## MELBOURNE

Continue north up Route 1 to find **Melbourne**, a turn-of-the-century city where the emphasis falls on history. The **Brevard Museum of Art and Science**, 1463 Highland Avenue, and the **Brevard Museum of History and Natural Science** in Cocoa both house visiting and permanent exhibitions and displays that tell the story of Florida from the Ice Age to the present. **Brevard Zoo**, 8225 N Wickham Road, has a Paws-On section to amuse children and adults alike and focuses on Latin American animals such as jaguars, llamas and monkeys. Open 10:00–17:00 daily.

At the **Space Coast stadium** you may be able to catch the Florida Marlin baseball team in training. This is also the place where you can enjoy many of the annual festivals which the city stages.

Just inland from Melbourne is **Palm Bay** and the **Turkey Creek Sanctuary**. A prime site for keen bird-watchers, this park is a major calling place for large flocks of **migratory birds**. Spring and autumn residents include rare woodpeckers and martins. **Manatees**, too, may be spotted from the 4000ft (1219m) boardwalk that takes visitors into the centre of the park and past some good bass fishing grounds. Call ahead on tel: (407) 952-3433 to find out when the park is open.

**Below:** *The Astronaut Memorial Planetarium and Observatory in Cocoa.*

## THE SPACE COAST

The Space Coast runs for 72 miles (116km) north–south along Florida's east coast. Although this area is a hub of high-tech activity, it is also a great family destination, a sporting mecca and an eco-friendly environment.

North of Melbourne lies the city of Cocoa, the beginning of the Space Coast. Here you will find the **Astronaut Memorial Planetarium and Observatory**, where visitors can study images of the surface of Mars, look at the rings of Saturn, or watch comets smashing down on to far-off planets. Call tel: (407) 634-3732 for opening times. Shoppers will enjoy the restored **Old Cocoa Village** area with its brick pavements and cobbled streets.

From Cocoa, cross over **Merritt Island** to reach **Cocoa Beach**, just south of Cape Canaveral. The Atlantic Ocean makes this a surfers' heaven and here you will find the famous (some would say infamous) **Ron Jon Surf Shop** – known by its outrageous billboards that line the coast. A must for shopaholics (even non-surfers will enjoy the spectacle), the shop is open 24 hours a day. A neighbouring park is filled with sand sculptures and includes an 820ft (250m) pier that doubles as a grandstand for shuttle launch viewing; this is a popular spot for fishermen.

### Cape Canaveral ★★★

The **NASA Kennedy Space Center** covers 140,000 acres (56,000ha). At its visitor centre, the public can admire a 6.2 million-pound (2,811,179kg) replica of the shuttle *Explorer* and visit the **Astronaut's Memorial** honouring the memory of American astronauts who have died. Their names are engraved into a polished granite disk which rotates to mirror the sun's movements.

**Above:** *The Ron Jon Surf Shop in Cocoa Beach has become a mecca for surfers.*

---

**MAN IN SPACE**

US President John F Kennedy sparked the space race in 1961. The Russians were ahead since one of their cosmonauts had already been in space, but Kennedy was determined: Americans would better them and send a man to the moon before the end of the decade. As a result, millions of dollars were pumped into **NASA**, culminating in the launch of **Apollo 11** and the historic moon landing in July 1969. The enormous cost incurred saw the industry going into decline until the launch of the reusable shuttle in 1981. This project, too, was initially fraught with problems. A fatal accident during the take-off of the **Challenger** mission in January 1986 caused a serious setback. The shuttle programme continues, albeit at a slower rate than the scientists would like.

### TURTLE TALK

From May–Sep, Space Coast beaches come alive as more than 6000 loggerhead, green and leatherback turtles arrive to lay their eggs. The females lumber ashore and dig nests. Each of the 2000-lb (907kg) animals will lay around 600 eggs (on average, only one nestling will make it to adult-hood). After laying their eggs, the nests are covered, and the exhausted giants make their way back to the sea.

Visitors can watch this night-time activity on tours run by the Sea Turtle Preservation Society, tel: (407) 676-1701 from 12:00–15:00.

New Smyrna Beach's portion of Canaveral National Sea-shore sponsors Turtle Walks during nesting season. Call 386-428-3384.

To learn more about sea turtle rehabilitation visit Ponce Inlet's Marine Science Center.

Exhibitions on the pre-Apollo Mercury and Gemini missions consume more of the visitor centre, as does the **IMAX Theater** with dramatic space-related films such as *The Dream is Alive,* including footage shot by astronauts aboard the Space Shuttle, and *L5: First City in Space* - a 3D exploration of the possible future colonisation of space.

The excellent bus tour allows visitors to spend as long as they wish at three fixed stops. The **LC39 Observation Gantry** brings views far across the space center and its launch pads. The **Apollo/Saturn V Center** has countless exhibits from the Apollo moon missions and a re-creation of the first landing. Finally, the **International Space Station Center** initiates visitors into the multi-nation project to create a permanent orbit-ing space base.

Space shuttles still blast off from the complex regu-larly and a provisional timetable is published every year. Dates may change due to bad weather or for technical reasons, but local tourist authorities are able to advise. Alternatively you can call tel: (+1) 407 867 4636 for recorded information or visit: www.kennedyspacecenter. com Call 800-USA-1969 for general information about the Space Coast.

## Titusville ★★

The most northerly city along this stretch of coastline, Titusville boasts a late-19th-century Main Street, now declared a **National Historic District**. It is also a vantage point for **shuttle launches**, and parking along the roadside is permitted up to 24 hours before take-off. Modern attractions include the **United States Astronaut Hall of Fame** and the **Valiant Air Command Warbird Museum**, which houses over 350 vintage aircraft, including Flying Tigers and C-47 Transporters, a Sopwith Camel and P-51 Mustang hardships. Flying displays are held annually in March. Open 10:00–18:00 daily, closed on public holidays.

**US Space Camp Florida**, open 09:00–17:00, allows children to experience the force of gravity and the thrill of aerial acrobatics. The **United States Space Walk of Fame**, filled with an abundance of memorabilia, lies alongside Indian River and overlooks the **Kennedy Space Center** – this is another favoured place for watching shuttle lift-offs.

**North Brevard Historical Museum** is worth a visit to see the handprints of the original Mercury astronauts, though nature lovers may prefer to explore the **Enchanted Forest**, a lush 400-acre (162ha) hardwood area with cabbage palms, saw palmettos, oaks and vines.

**Opposite:** *The Astronaut Hall of Fame in Titusville.*
**Below:** *Children meet a real 'moonwalker' at the Kennedy Space Center.*

Almost opposite Titusville on a spit of land which runs south from New Smyrna Beach to Cape Canaveral is Merritt Island, shared by NASA and the **Merritt Island National Wildlife Refuge**. One of the state's leading wildlife viewing areas, it adjoins the Canaveral National Seashore with its 24-mile (39km) beach. There are ranger-led **tours** of the reserve, observation towers for bird-watching and a visitor centre with information about the area. The refuge covers about 220 sq miles (572km²), or 140,000 acres (56,657ha) and claims to provide a home for more endangered species than any other reserve in the United

**DAYTONA SPEEDWAY**

Races are held from February to the end of October. The first is the **Sunbank 24**, a 24-hour race for sports cars. Trials start in mid-February for the **Daytona 500** stock car race – the classic of the year. By March it is the turn of the bikes, with half a million enthusiasts attending a **Bike Week Festival**. The **Pepsi 400** sees the cars back in July, followed by the **Daytona Pro-Am** in October. The **Bikoberfest** is the year's finale with races and shows.

States. Manatees, bald eagles and loggerhead turtles can all be found here. Both Merritt and Canaveral have boardwalks to take visitors through the dunes and shady hummocks (note that it is against the law to walk on the dunes). Surfing and beachcombing are particularly rewarding along this stretch of coast, though swimming is not recommended due to strong currents and the presence of stinging jellyfish. The best time for bird lovers to visit is winter, when huge flocks of migratory birds mill about.

### New Smyrna Beach ★
On the way north to Daytona Beach lies the quaint town of New Smyrna Beach. Founded in 1770, New Smyrna Beach was once the largest colony under British rule in the New World. It was developed by a number of enterprising Minorcan, Greek and Italian immigrants. The scenic **Spruce Creek Canoe Trail** starts and ends at Moody Bridge near New Smyrna Beach; its two loops leading through hardwood forests and salt marsh.

### THE DAYTONA BEACH AREA
The Daytona Beach area has been a family holiday destination for more than a century. The popular resort area which stretches from Ormond-By-The-Sea to Ponce Inlet continues to strive to be an all-around family destination. The areas newest attractions, the **Marine Science Center** and **Ocean Walk Shoppes** – an oceanfront dining, shopping and entertainment complex – complement its growing list of family-friendly offerings.

Visitors can drive or park along 11 of the 23 miles (37km) of sands that helped **Sir Malcolm Campbell** into the record books. A fare is charged to obtain vehicle access to the beach. Vehicles are permitted to drive at just 10mph (16kph) – it is quicker by bicycle. Up to 500ft (152m) wide in places, the

**Below:** *The New Smyrna Sugar Mill Ruins are a peaceful haven.*

sandy beach is the focus of life in the city. Beach vendors sell everything from hot dogs to T-shirts and you can hire sunbeds and bicycles. Surfers head out early to catch the first waves of the day, while other water-sports enthusiasts may enjoy boating, para-sailing or jet-skiing. Deep-sea fishing charters are available in Ponce Inlet at the southernmost tip of the Daytona Beach area.

**Above:** *Cars cruise along Daytona Beach, famous for its stock car and bike races.*

Spectators wander along the famous **Boardwalk**, which offers miniature golf, game arcades, fast-food outlets and shops. Equally attractive is the **Daytona Beach Pier**. Those wanting a really good view of the area should take a ride in the overhead gondola. **Ocean Walk Shoppes** is the latest addition to the Boardwalk area and features a 10-screen movie theater, unique clothing stores, and family-friendly restaurants and eateries.

Shoppers should head to Daytona Beach's two weekly markets. The **Farmers Market** on City Island along **Riverfront Marketplace** – the city's historic downtown shopping dining and entertainment district – sells fresh fruit and seafood, caught or grown locally. Chefs from many of the town's 400 restaurants do their shopping here. Riverfront Marketplace is also home to a chocolate factory, gift shops, antique malls, restaurants, nightclubs, a chandler and an historical museum. The **Daytona Flea Market** presents 40 acres (17ha) of haggler's paradise. Everything from food to antiques is available here, including some real bargains as well as mountains of tat.

The Daytona Beach area is home to several museums. The **Southeast Museum of Photography**, at 1200 W. International Speedway Blvd, Building 100, is Florida's only museum exclusively dedicated to photography. The 10,000ft² (930m²) museum is one of only 12 museums of

---

### PARTY TIME

**February** • Grant Seafood Festival, Melbourne: feast on oysters, clams and crabs.
**March** • Florida Marlins Spring Training, Melbourne: catch a pre-season game. Port Canaveral Seafood Festival, Titusville: fresh fish and gallons of chowder. Valiant Air Command Warbird Air Show, Titusville: a flying spectacular featuring Warplanes of all ages.
**Easter Weekend** • Easter Surfing Festival, Cocoa Beach.
**April** • Indian River Festival, Titusville: bikini contests, river raft races and celebrity look-alike competitions. Melbourne Art Festival: almost 300 artists gather to display local arts and crafts.

**Right:** *The watchtower on the promenade at Daytona Beach.*
**Opposite:** *Ponce de León Lighthouse towers above its surroundings.*

its kind in the US and one of fewer than 30 in the world. SMP exhibitions have travelled to such respected institutions as the Metropolitan Museum of Art, The Carpenter Center at Harvard, and the Pitt-Rivers Museum at Oxford. Open 10:00–16:00 Monday, Wednesday–Friday; 11:00–19:00 Tuesday; and 13:00–17:00 Saturday–Sunday.

The **Museum of Arts and Sciences** on 1040 Museum Blvd is worth visiting for its amazing collection of Cuban art brought to the area by former Cuban president Fulgencio Batista, who had a holiday home in the area and bequeathed his collection to the museum. This is also the place to see the impressive skeleton of a prehistoric giant ground sloth measuring 13ft (4m), which was found in the area. Open 09:00–16:00 Tuesday–Friday, 12:00–17:00 Saturday; closed Sunday, Monday and public holidays.

The performing arts scene is alive and well in Daytona Beach! The city is the official American summer home of the **London Symphony Orchestra** (LSO). In fact, the LSO has performed intact more times in Daytona Beach than any other place in the world outside of London. Since 1966, the LSO has been the featured performer at Daytona Beach's **Florida International Festival** – a 17-day entertainment extravaganza that features a variety of world-renowned performance artists. The festival is held biennially in July. Daytona Beach is also home to **Seaside Music Theater**, an acclaimed professional theatre com-

# The East Coast at a Glance

**The Villa Bed & Breakfast**, tel (386) 248-2020, web: www.thevillabb.com One of the city's superior small lodging options with just 4 rooms and a beach-front location.

## MID-RANGE
**Mayan Inn Beachfront**, 103 South Ocean Ave, tel: (386) 252-2378, web: www.BWMayanInn.com Complimentary breakfasts; great views over the ocean.
**Treasure Island Resort**, 2025 S. Atlantic Ave, tel: (386) 255-8371, web: www.oceansresorts.com On South Daytona beach, with 3 pools.

## BUDGET
**Cardinal Motel**, 738 N Atlantic Avenue, Daytona Beach, tel: (386) 252-1035, fax: 257-3571, toll-free: 800 555-2819. Weekly and monthly accom-modation rates are available.
**Copacabana**, 1201 S. Atlantic Ave, tel: (386) 252-1452, web: www.realpages.com/copacabana Family owned and operated for five decades, heated pool and beach location.

## WHERE TO EAT
The central East Coast has a wide variety of eateries to suit every budget.
This area prides itself on its seafood. Annual festivals celebrate oyster catches, seafood and river fish.

*Vero Beach*
Try out the excellent seafood at **Ocean Grill**, 1050 Beachland Blvd, tel: (772) 231-5409.
Or go for authentic American at **Sonya's**, 9250 Island Grove Ter, tel: (772) 234 2180 – reservations recommended.

*Cocoa Beach*
**Bernard's Surf**, 2 S Atlantic Ave, tel: (321) 783-2401. Excellent seafood, dinner only.

*Daytona Beach*
**Lighthouse Landing**, 4931 Peninsula Drive, tel: (386) 761-9271.
A good spot to sip cocktails and watch the sun go down before enjoying the fresh seafood.
**Cap'n Coty's**, 333 Beville Road, S Daytona, tel: (386) 761-1333. Casual and very friendly; low-cost seafood and steak house.

## TOURS AND EXCURSIONS
**Kennedy Space Center**, tel: (321) 449-4444, web: www.kennedyspacecenter.com See launch pads, shuttle engines and space travel artefacts.
**Adventure Kayak of Cocoa Beach**, tel: (321) 480-8632. Tour the coastline and catch glimpses of dolphins and manatees.
**A Day Away Kayaking & Fitness**, tel: (321) 268-2655. Guided kayak tours on the Space Coast's diverse waterways; meals included. Kayak rentals. Outfitter service.

## USEFUL CONTACTS
**Daytona Beach Area Convention and Visitors Bureau**, 126 E Orange Ave, Daytona Beach FL32114, tel: (386) 255-0415, web: www.daytonabeach.com
**Space Coast Visitors Center**, 3445 Cheney Hwy, Titusville, tel: (321) 269-9345, web: www.spacecoastvisitorscenter.com
**Indian River County Chamber of Commerce**, Tourism Division, 1216 21st St, Vero Beach FL32960, tel: (772) 567 4391, web: www.indianriverchamber.com

| DAYTONA BEACH | J | F | M | A | M | J | J | A | S | O | N | D |
|---|---|---|---|---|---|---|---|---|---|---|---|---|
| AVERAGE TEMP. °F | 58 | 59 | 64 | 69 | 75 | 79 | 81 | 81 | 79 | 73 | 66 | 60 |
| AVERAGE TEMP. °C | 14 | 15 | 18 | 21 | 24 | 26 | 27 | 27 | 26 | 23 | 19 | 16 |
| HOURS OF SUN DAILY | 12 | 12 | 12 | 13 | 13 | 14 | 14 | 14 | 13 | 12 | 12 | 12 |
| RAINFALL in | 3 | 3 | 3 | 2 | 3 | 6 | 5 | 6 | 6 | 4 | 3 | 3 |
| RAINFALL mm | 76 | 76 | 76 | 51 | 76 | 152 | 127 | 152 | 152 | 102 | 76 | 76 |
| DAYS OF RAINFALL | 7 | 8 | 8 | 7 | 9 | 13 | 14 | 12 | 11 | 9 | 7 | 7 |

# 5

# The Northeast

An area of immense contrast, the beautiful Northeast region contains both the oldest and youngest of Florida. This was where the Spaniards first gained a strong foothold in the state, and also where the first skyscraper was completed in 1901.

**Jacksonville** is the business capital of the region and covers the largest area of any city in the United States. Divided by the **St Johns River**, the city is a mix of modern skyscrapers and historical sites. It is also home to the country's largest brewery and gourmands will enjoy the riverside restaurants and cafés that give Jacksonville such a rich cosmopolitan flavour.

To the north lies **Fernandina Beach**, one of the nation's oldest cities, while to the south lies **St Augustine** where the oldest schoolhouse vies for attention with the oldest shop, the oldest church and the oldest fort.

The Northeast has miles of sensational beaches and picturesque lakes and rivers. Its proximity to Georgia and the rest of the United States helped the area develop as a tourist destination back in the last century. Today, although many visitors drive on south, there is still plenty to stop for.

Wildlife abounds in the deep forests and wide lakes, and **St Augustine Alligator Farm** is one of the most popular attractions. The proud history of the area is brought to life with a series of colourful festivals and realistic re-enactments throughout the year, while the younger cities contain a wealth of cultural activity and a wide range of shopping opportunities.

GEORGIA
Tallahassee · Jacksonville

FLORIDA

GULF OF
MEXICO

Miami

### DON'T MISS

**\*\*\* The Spanish Quarter, St Augustine:** restored to its former 17th-century glory.
**\*\* The Riverwalk, Jacksonville:** shops and bars, many restaurants and street entertainment.
**\*\* St Augustine Alligator Farm:** birds, monkeys and tortoises, as well as alligators.
**\*\* Amelia Island beaches:** some of the very best in the Northeast, with high dunes.
**\*\* Marjorie Kinnan Rawlings' house:** Cross Creek home of the Pulitzer prize-winning novelist.

**Opposite:** *The 'Stars and Stripes' flies out in St Augustine.*

## St Augustine

With more than 60 different historic sites and attractions, St Augustine has plenty to offer. The city claims to be North America's oldest town although this title has, in the past, been disputed by Pensacola in northwest Florida. What is clear is that St Augustine is the oldest continuously inhabited town in the United States. It was first settled in 1565 by the Spanish and several of their original buildings can still be visited today. A host of annual festivals helps to retain its historical appeal and brings the old world back to life. To explore the historic zone in the centre of town, either take a horse-drawn carriage tour or, better still, venture forth on foot. A good place to start is at the old **City Gate** (top of **St George Street**). Not only is this close to the main visitor information centre, but it also adjoins the **Castillo de San Marcos National Monument**, built by the Spanish in 1672. The unique material they used was *coquina*, a soft limestone made from broken shells and coral. The fort is surrounded by a moat and comes complete with turrets and walls 16ft (5m) thick. Visit the garrison rooms and try to catch one of the artillery demonstrations that are held on the gun deck.

At Number 14 St George Street you will find the quaint **Oldest Wooden Schoolhouse**, built before the American Revolution out of cypress and red cedar wood. A little further down the road is the **Spanish Quarter**, a fully restored and functional historical village with craftspeople making candles, weaving or spinning. All the items made here are used to continue the upkeep of the Quarter.

*Map: St Augustine*

JACKSONVILLE
Ripley's Believe It or Not! Museum
Castillo Dr
Castillo de San Marcos National Monument
Old City Gate
Museum Theater
Oldest Wooden Schoolhouse
Orange
Spanish Quarter Museum
Saragossa
Cuna
Carrera
Hypolita
CASABLANCA INN
Treasury
Valencia
Basilica Cathedral of St Augustine
Plaza de la Constitution
Bridge of Lions
Flagler College
Cathedral Pl
CASA MONICA
Potter's Wax Museum
King
Castle
Artillery
Zorayda
Lightner Museum
Oldest Store Museum
Cadiz
La Quinta
Cedar
De Soto
Matanzas Bay
Bravo
Bridge
Oldest House
0   250 yd
0   250 m
San Sebastian
Ponce de Leon Blvd
Ribera
Malaga
Sevilla
Spanish
St George
Cordova
Charlotte
Avenida Menendez
Marine
Aviles
Bravo
M L King
Cordova
Washington
San Marco Ave
AILEANOR LANE
ALLIGATOR FARM
N

At the point where St George Street and Cathedral Place meet, stands the lovely **Basilica Cathedral of St Augustine.** This has undergone various renovations and remodelling, particularly after a fire in 1887. But it still houses parish records dating back to 1594, the oldest known written records in the United States.

**Above:** *The Oldest Wooden Schoolhouse dates back to British colonial times.*
**Opposite:** *Inside the quaint Oldest Store Museum.*

The **Plaza de la Constitution** was the centre of the original settlement and today houses a monument to the Spanish constitution of 1812 and a statue of Juan Ponce de León, the first European to set foot in Florida, back in 1513. The **National Archaeological Park** on Magnolia Avenue commemorates his quest to find the Fountain of Eternal Youth (*see* p. 10).

Turn left off St George Street on to King Street and then right into Artillery Lane to find the **Oldest Store Museum**, displaying some 100,000 items that would have been sold at the turn of the century, such as lace-up corsets, medicine containing 90% alcohol(!) and red flannel underwear. The shop attendants all wear authentic costumes. A little further down the lane is the **Oldest House**, which, under the auspices of the local historical society, has been preserved to reflect the life of its various owners; each room's decor illustrating a different era of its occupation.

Back on King Street you'll find **Zorayda Castle**, a reproduction of Spain's Alhambra, with treasures from around the world. The **Lightner Museum**, a few doors along, occupies the former Hotel Alcazar and exhibits 19th-century collectibles. Antique music boxes are a speciality and the attendants happily give demos.

The **Mission of Nombre de Dios**, on San Marco Avenue, is believed to have been the site where America's first mass was celebrated.

**ST AUGUSTINE ALTERNATIVES**

**Potter's Wax Museum**, 17 King Street: contains 170 historical figures, a wax workshop and shop.
**Ripley's Believe It or Not!** at 19 San Marco Avenue: unusual museum filled with oddities from around the world, an amusing place to while away an hour or two.
**St Augustine Alligator Farm**, 999 Anastasia Blvd: be sure to catch the alligator show when a keeper gets terrifyingly close to the jaws of the animals; the only place to house all 23 species of the world's crocodiles and alligators. Call ahead for show times on tel: (877) 966-7275. Open daily 09:00–18:00.

**Above:** *The modern sky-scrapers of Jacksonville overlook the St Johns River.*
**Opposite:** *Jacksonville is home to a large brewing industry.*

---

**THE BEACHES**

**St Augustine:** the start of more than 20 miles (30km) of beach running north-wards. Extremely popular, particularly at weekends.
**Ponte Vedra:** million-dollar homes and golf courses line this stunning beach, the most southerly of the Jacksonville Beaches. Public access to the sand is limited but worth the hunt for crowd-free sunning and shell collecting.
**Jacksonville:** a mix of commuters who travel into the city and tourists wanting to enjoy the beach.
**Neptune:** very much quieter, mostly a residential area.
**Atlantic:** lively area hemmed by restaurants, bars and disco. Great surfing.

---

## JACKSONVILLE

Named after General Andrew Jackson back in 1822, this city began as a tiny town called Cowford nestling on the banks of the St Johns River. Today it spreads out over the largest area of any city in the United States, is one of the most vibrant and, although bypassed frequently on tours of the state, has plenty to offer. Some of the downtown area can be explored by water taxi and by a futuristic mono-rail, but you need a car to reach the other attractions. It's worth planning trips carefully to avoid spending the day criss-crossing the river.

The **north side** of the downtown area is home to the city's Convention Center and **River City Playhouse**, staging both adults' and children's theatre, as well as the Courthouse, City Hall and Chamber of Commerce.

The **Florida Theatre** on E Forsyth Street is considered the cultural heart of the city and stages more than 100 events annually. The **Cummer Gallery**, on the northwest bank of the river on Riverside Avenue, houses a fine art gallery, displays of early Meissen porcelain and an art education centre. Open 10:00–16:00 Tuesday–Friday, noon–17:00 Saturday and 14:00–17:00 Sunday.

On Zoo Road and bordering the Trout River is **Jacksonville Zoo** (open 09:00–17:00 daily). It houses 700 animal species, many in enclosures that imitate their nat-ural habitat as in the African veld section.

Only a short distance away is the **Anheuser–Busch Brewery** on Busch Drive, where visitors can join a con-ducted tour of the plant to learn more about the beer-making process.

Afterwards enjoy a brew in the sampling room of what is reputed to be the largest brewery in the United States. Open 09:00–16:00, Monday–Saturday.

## Jacksonville Landing *

The Landing on Independence Drive is a collection of shops and restaurants, many of which overlook the river, and has entertainers performing in the fountain plaza. It can be reached by water taxi.

The **Riverwalk** on the south bank extends for some 1.2 miles (2km), has a fountain that is lit at night, a marina, water taxi station, restaurants, shops and street vendors. It leads to the **Jacksonville Museum of Science and History**, which incorporates an interactive Children's Museum. Call tel: (904) 396-7062 for opening times.

The **Alexander Brest Museum**, on the campus of Jacksonville University, houses exhibits of Steuben glass, Boehm porcelain and pre-Columbian artefacts. The **Jacksonville Art Museum** on Center Drive has oriental porcelain and artefacts dating from 3000BC to AD1500.

**Fort Caroline National Memorial** on 12713 Fort Caroline Road contains a model of the original fort. Open daily 09:00–17:00, closed Christmas.

---

### AMELIA ISLAND

The only part of the United States to have flown eight different flags, this 13-mile (21km) island has escaped much of the commercialism apparent elsewhere in Florida. The charming main town, Fernandina, was once the hotbed of pirates.

The **Museum of History** and **St Peter's Episcopal Church**, which served as a school for freed slaves, are worth a visit. Three miles (5km) north is the **Fort Clinch State Park** with a brick fort built by Americans to protect Georgia from further British intrusion after the 1812 war. The fort was only used during the 1847 Civil War when it was occupied by the Confederacy.

### DATES TO REMEMBER

**1562** French Huguenots establish a colony at Fort Caroline on St John's River.
**1565** Pedro Menéndez de Avilés founds St Augustine.
**1727** Oldest surviving house in St Augustine is built.
**1822** Town of Cowford is renamed Jacksonville after General Andrew Jackson.
**1832** William J Mills becomes first mayor of Jacksonville.
**1864** Florida's only major Civil War fight, the Battle of Olustee, takes place.
**1901** A huge fire destroys downtown Jacksonville.
**1908** Jacksonville starts to gain a reputation as the winter film capital with the opening of a major studio.

**Below:** *The entrance of the recently opened Harn Museum in Gainesville.*

## GAINESVILLE

Tourism officials around Gainesville call the area 'The Original Florida' because of its small towns filled with history, its bubbling springs and tiny fishing villages. Gainesville, the centre of the region, is the cultural capital of the area, home of the **University of Florida**. The campus houses the **Florida Museum of Natural History**, which contains fascinating displays taking you from dinosaurs to virtual reality. Open 10:00–17:00 Tuesday–Saturday, 13:00–17:00 Sunday.

The **Harn Museum** on Hull Road is one of Florida's latest institutions, exhibiting African, American and pre-Columbian artefacts across 62,000ft² (19,000m²) of gallery space. The **Fred Bear Museum** on Archer Road is dedicated to the art of archery and contains artefacts dating back to the Stone Age. Open 10:00–18:00 daily.

Be sure to visit beautiful **Kanapaha Botanical Gardens** on 63rd Boulevard. This is the second-largest garden in Florida and claims to be the most diverse.

In the downtown area indoor cultural activities take place at the **Center for the Performing Arts** which opened in 1992. Elsewhere, Constans Theater offers student productions that have been sponsored by the Florida Theater Department, while the Gainesville Community Theater puts on shows with other promising local talent. The Hippodrome State Theater by contrast, presents plays with international and national stars and is surrounded by pavement cafés, studios, bars and clubs.

South of Gainesville, down US441, the **Paynes Prairie State Preserve** is extremely popular with campers, hikers, horse-riders and canoeists. This area was once home to native Americans and artefacts found here date back to 7000BC. Some buffalo, horses and alligators are among the permanent residents.

# 6
# The Northwest

The Northwest, or **Panhandle** as it is often called, is bordered by Alabama to the north and Georgia to the northeast. This area is also known as the **Emerald Coast** after the vivid greens and rich blues of the sea that contrast starkly with its white beaches.

The Northwest has had a totally different development pattern from the rest of the state. The first area to be won over by the Americans, it was also the most closely involved in the Civil War. Industry and agriculture have been linked to northern neighbouring states rather than the citrus belt to the south.

Early settlers tried their luck in **Pensacola**, but a combination of disease and hurricanes forced them out and it was St Augustine that became the first established colony in Florida. The two cities have since argued fiercely over which is the oldest settlement in the United States, which led to **Tallahassee** becoming state capital as a compromise. Tallahassee is closer to Atlanta than to Miami, and magnolias and live oaks rather than palm trees colour the scenery.

Beyond the historic towns, the region is studded with springs, forest reserves, tunnels, caves and coastal parks, including the **Florida Caverns State Park** with its intriguing calcite formations. Other interesting parks include the **Natural Bridge Battlefield State Historic Site**, where Confederate soldiers once battled to save Tallahassee from falling into enemy hands, and the **Torreya State Park** with its 150ft (46m) bluffs towering high above the Apalachicola River. (Website: www.floridastateparks.org)

**DON'T MISS**

*** Cedar Key:** a tranquil reminder of times gone by.
** North Hill Preservation District:** dating back to Pensacola's origins.
** Panama City Beach:** a 27-mile (43km) stretch of dazzling, fine white sand beach considered one of the best in the world.
** 22nd floor of the New Capitol, Tallahassee:** a fine view of the capital city.
** National Museum of Naval Aviation:** one of the world's largest aircraft museums.

**Opposite:** *One of the many spectacular sunsets on the northwestern Panhandle.*

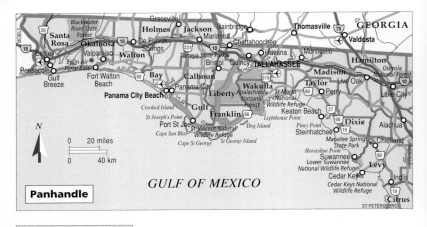

**Panhandle**

GULF OF MEXICO

## CLIMATE

The **summer** months of **July** and **August** are **hottest** with temperatures reaching an average of 92°F (33°C). The spring months from April to June can average a chillier 63°F (17°C), while winter temperatures can fall to an average 44°F (7°C) between January and March. **Hurricanes** hit this coastline after travelling across the Gulf – they are most likely in **August** and **September**.

## PENSACOLA

First inhabited in 1559 by a group of Spanish settlers headed by Don Tristan De Luna, Pensacola is extremely proud of its history and the fact that it has been ruled by five nations. The Spanish, after abandoning their original settlement, returned in 1698 to build a fort at the site of the present day Naval Air Station. Subsequently, control of the city shifted uneasily between the Spanish and British, until it became part of the United States in 1821 with General Andrew Jackson as its first governor.

The **Civil War** divided the city, with Southerners holding Fort McRee and the Yankees holed up in Fort Pickens on the offshore island of Santa Rosa (today's Pensacola Beach, which is the site of most of the resort hotels). The 'rebels' finally fled and Pensacola was taken for the North. In 1886, little **Fort Pickens** became the city's first real tourist destination as eager crowds flocked to catch a glimpse of the prominent and feared Apache chief, **Geronimo**.

## Seville, Palafox and North Hill ★★

Starting at the west end of **Three Mile Bridge** you first reach the historic district of **Seville**. Once the centre of the Spanish town, it is now a mix of Creole (some dating from the 1780s) and Victorian homes – many of which have been restored and converted into shops or restaurants. The centre of this area, **Seville Square**, is surrounded by live oaks and provides the setting for the annual Greater Gulfcoast Arts Festival, held on the first weekend of November, which attracts in excess of 100,000 people, as well as the Jazz- or Springfest, a three-day event in April. Off to one side is Alcaniz Street with St Michael's Cemetery containing several thousand graves, some over 200 years old.

To the west lies **Palafox Historic District**. Wrought iron balconies grace Spanish architecture in what was once the commercial district of old Pensacola. Walking on, you reach **North Hill Preservation District**, an upper-class neighbourhood from the 1870s with examples of Queen Anne, neoclassical, Mediterranean and Tudor Revival architecture. It was built on the site of an old fortress, and people still find cannonballs in their gardens.

South of North Hill lies **Historic Pensacola Village** (open 10:00–16:00 Monday–Saturday; closed on state holidays), commemorating the city's past 200 years in a series of exhibitions. The **Museum of Industry** concentrates on the economic past, while old **Christ Church** houses the Pensacola Historical Museum. Other sites include the Julee Cottage Museum of Black History, Lavalle House and Quina House. The **Pensacola Museum of Art** on Jefferson Street once served as a prison. Further down the street, the old city hall has become the **TT Wentworth Jr Florida State Museum** and now houses a very interesting Kidstown display on the second floor, guaranteed to delight children of all ages.

**Opposite:** *Many of Pensacola's houses date back to the 1780s.*
**Below:** *The National Museum of Naval Aviation in Pensacola.*

**PERDIDO KEY**

Protecting Pensacola to
the south, Perdido Key has
become a popular tourist
destination in its own right,
with bridge connections to
both Florida and Alabama.
Most tourist development is
in high-rise condominiums
and hotels overlooking the
Gulf or the Old River.
Part of the Gulf Islands
National Seashore, the
island contains the **Perdido
Key State Park** and **Big
Lagoon State Park** with a
40ft (12m) lookout tower
for bird-spotting over the
marshes.

## ALONG THE COAST

The past few years has seen development of the resorts
along the coast between Pensacola and Panama City,
Fort Walton and Destin, in particular, have enjoyed
growth with large resort complexes opening on the spectacular beaches that make up the Emerald Coast.

## PANAMA CITY BEACH

Citizens of Panama City Beach are incredibly proud of their
magnificently white soft beach, and with good reason. In
1994 the stretch of beach at St Andrews State Park was
declared the best in America by the University of
Maryland's laboratory for coastal research. The young
crowd agrees, and each spring some 500,000 American students descend for their traditional spring break. Made
legendary by Hollywood, spring breaks are known for
riotous behaviour and some Florida cities have been eager
to persuade the students to move on. Panama City Beach,
however, extends a warm welcome while encouraging con-
sideration for other visitors. Panama City Beach is also a
favourite with families because of its lower costs, excellent
facilities and more than 300 days of sunshine per annum,
as well as a growing reputation for tasty seafood dishes.

### Local Attractions ★★

The area is divided by St Andrews Bay with Panama
City lying to the east and Panama City Beach 5 miles

**DESTIN/FORT WALTON**

Spread along 24 miles (38km)
of sugar-white sand coast
with brilliant green waters,
the Destin/Fort Walton beach
towns deserve the **Emerald
Coast** accolade.
With the 100-fathom curve
closer to shore in this
area than anywhere else,
Destin–Fort Walton has the
speediest deep-water access
in the Gulf and some of the
best shells around. Fishing and
seafood are excellent, sailing
and water sports abound.
The area is also renowned for
golf, with 545 holes designed
around woods and wetlands.

**Left:** *Interesting exhibits at the Museum of Man in the Sea, Panama City.*
**Opposite:** *Fort Walton Beach, one of many stunning white beaches along the Emerald Coast.*
**Below:** *The Emerald Coast is great sailing territory.*

(8km) west. Most visitor attractions are on the beach. **Gulf World** on 15412 Front Beach Road has four shows daily featuring dolphins, penguins and sea lions. There is also a tropical garden, scuba diving and shark feeding demonstrations. Call tel: (850) 234-5271 for opening times. **Coconut Creek Family Fun Park** is also on Front Beach Road, tel: (850) 234 2625.

Another attraction is the **Bay County's Junior Museum** on 1731 Jenks Avenue, where children can play Indian games and explore a tepee, log cabin and a pioneer village, as well as a nature trail. Open 13:00–16:30 Tue–Fri, 10:00–16:00 Sat, 13:00–16:00 Sun.

The **Visual Art Center of Northwest Florida** is on E Fourth Street. Exhibits change every six weeks and visitors are encouraged to join classes or workshops.

The award-winning **St Andrews State Park** at the southeastern tip of Panama City Beach, covers 1260 acres (510ha). It has two fishing piers, water-sports facilities and picnic sites, and its beaches are a paradise for beachcombers; there are also camping facilities.

### TALLAHASSEE

Billed as 'Florida with a Southern accent', Tallahassee is a town of historic homes set amid plantations and magnolia trees, bustling with politics and commerce. It also makes a good base for exploring nearby scenic attractions and soaking up the plentiful history and culture of the area.

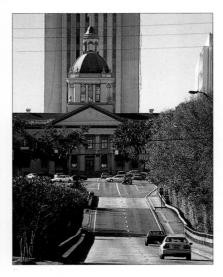

**Above:** *The new towers above the Old Capitol building in Tallahassee.*
**Opposite:** *The fine façade of the Supreme Court.*

## City Hall, the Old and the New Capitol *

The **Old Capitol** is situated on the corner of the Apalachee Parkway and S Monroe Street and was opened in 1845 when the city was declared the state capital. Altered in 1902, the stately building has retained its magnificent stained-glass dome, as well as the impressive rotunda and political chambers. It takes about 45 minutes to view all the exhibits inside, outlining Florida's history and political evolution. The **New Capitol** comes alive during the political session (March–May). The 22nd floor offers a panoramic view of the city and on clear days you can see as far as the Gulf of Mexico. Self-guided tours are available during regular New Capitol hours, 08:00–17:00 weekdays, closed weekends. Free guided group tours may be booked in advance by calling (8500 488-6167. The Visitors Info Center on the plaza level is open 08:00–17:00 weekdays, closed weekends.

Near the New Capitol, two blocks west on S Bronough Street, is the **Museum of Florida History** where recovered Spanish treasure vies for attention with prehistoric finds. War relics and a steamboat complete the collection.

### TALLAHASSEE FACTS

*Tallahassee* is the native American word for 'land of old fields' or 'abandoned villages', and today supports a population of 133,731. It lies in the eastern time zone and, like Rome, is surrounded by seven hills. The only uncaptured Confederate capital east of the Mississippi, the city preserves the site of the Battle of Natural Bridge.

Open 09:00–16:30 Monday–Friday; 10:00–16:30 Saturday; 12.00–16:30 Sunday and holidays. For more information check http://dhr.dos.state.fl.us/museum

Further north on neighbouring N Adams Street is the Georgian-style **Governor's Mansion**. Its state rooms are filled with fine antiques and gifts from abroad. Only five rooms are open to the public, tours of which are available during legislative session and Christmas holidays. Call tel: (850) 488-4661 for times.

## Museums and Archaeological Sites *

Head out of the downtown area on E Park Avenue to the **Knott House Museum**, built by a free Black builder in 1843, which today houses a large collection of gilt-framed mirrors. Rhymes written on silk ribbons by its eccentric owner are attached to the furniture. This was the site of the formal declaration of emancipation of North Florida slaves in 1865, officially freeing all remaining slaves in the state.

The city is an easy drive from America's greatest concentration of plantations – 71 estates scattered across Southern Georgia, close to Thomasville.

On a hill to the west of town near the intersection of Tennessee Street and W Mission Road lies the **San Luis Archaeological and Historic Site**, home of Apalachee

**WALKABOUT**

Tallahassee has at least three easy walking routes to take in the main sights. The downtown area is also served by a free trolley. Free walking and trolley maps are available at the **Tallahassee Area Visitor Information Center**, New Capitol Building.
**Downtown:** start from the New Capitol for a taste of the city as political and retail centre with varied architecture and shopping.
**Park Avenue Historic District Tour:** explore the city's historic churches, old cemetery and the parks which were once a dirt clearing to protect the city from attack.
**Calhoun Street Historic District Tour:** has the largest concentration of historic homes and was once known as Gold Dust Street, due to its many wealthy residents.

**Above:** *St Mark's lighthouse was built with stone from a 17th-century fort.*

Indians and Spanish settlers from 1656 to 1704. An annual heritage festival includes costumed re-enactments and there are also regular excavations around the 50-acre (20ha) plot. Another historical re-enactment takes place at the **De Soto Archaeological Site** off Lafayette Street, the place where Hernando de Soto and his troops celebrated the first Christmas in America, back in 1539.

The **Tallahassee Museum of History and Natural Science** on Museum Drive has native red wolves, Florida panthers and alligators living on 52 acres (21ha) alongside an 1880s farm exhibit and a plantation home.

### State Parks ★★

Tallahassee is surrounded by numerous state parks, including the **Florida Caverns State Park** near Marianna, which provides hourly tours through caves and caverns filled with spectacular calcite formations: soda straws, stalactites, stalagmites, columns, flowstones and draperies. Open 08:00–sunset daily. This is the only cavern, visitors can walk into as the rest are underwater caves.

The **Torreya State Park** is the site of Gregory House, a former cotton plantation; the surrounding park is filled with the rare torreya evergreen, as well as yew trees and the US champion-winged elm. Open 08:00–sunset daily, house tours 10:00 Monday–Friday, and 10:00, 14:00, 16:00 on Saturday and Sunday.

The **Apalachicola National Forest** includes more than 500,000 acres (202,347ha) of untouched native forest and lies just 10 miles (17km) south of the city. Tallahassee is also surrounded by lakes, among them Lake Jackson, Lake Bradford and Lake Talquin.

---

### SOUTH FROM TALLAHASSEE

A Spanish mission and 17th-century fort made **St Marks** a powerful place. Stones from the fort were used to build a lighthouse which is still in operation today. A later Civil War fort here was separately occupied by each of the opposing sides.

Once the third-largest cotton port on the Gulf Coast, nearby **Apalachicola** served as a base for blockade runners during the Civil War. It is now the state's most important oyster fishery – and home to the John Gorrie State Museum, dedicated to the man who invented fridges, ice-makers and air conditioners (see page 14). To the north and west is the **Apalachicola National Forest** and the **Torreya State Park**, named after the rare 'torreya' tree which is said to have grown in the garden of Eden.

# 7
# The West Coast

Hostile natives and insect-infested swamps once saw this area frequented only by buccaneers in search of a hide out. Florida's West Coast is relatively new territory for European visitors too, but beaches, resort areas, private islands, and a wealth of culture have started attracting tourists.

What Flagler did for the east coast in terms of development, magnate **Henry Plant** achieved here on the West Coast. Many elegant Victorian homes in Tampa and along the coastal strip owe their origins to Plant, who brought the railroad and, with it, industry and wealth.

**Tampa** lies at the heart of the West Coast development, characterized by its industrial history, port and tourist attractions. Nearby ethnic enclaves add their own inimitable style to the region; a Czech community in Brooksville holds regular strudel bakes in an effort to retain the ways of their fatherland.

The **St Petersburg** area has stunning beaches and spectacular sunsets. A string of islands leads down to **Sarasota**, where classical music mixes with the razzmatazz of the circus. The West Coast even has its own **Venice** – criss-crossed with canals and home to the world's only clown college. Further down the coast wildlife replaces city glitz as the main attraction, with **Fort Myers** and **Naples** surrounded by national parks and the vast **Everglades**. Many Americans have bought homes in this area, making it as rich and exclusive as its east coast counterpart, Palm Beach. Visitors always receive a warm welcome, whether driving through or staying awhile.

## DON'T MISS

\*\*\* **Sunshine Skyway:** enjoy the views of the islands and Tampa Bay.
\*\*\* **Busch Gardens:** thrill of roller coasters tempered with wildlife and gardens.
\*\*\* **Ybor City:** Cuban life, history and entertainment.
\*\* **Corkscrew Swamp Sanctuary:** a wilderness of 11,000 acres (4452ha), inhabited by alligators, bobcats and otters.
\*\* **John and Mable Ringling complex:** amazing combination put together by this famous circus couple.

**Opposite:** *Fun in the sun at Tigertail Beach on Marco Island.*

## TAMPA BAY AND SURROUNDS
## Tampa ★

Native Americans first discovered the natural attractions of Tampa, its harbour protected by the sandbanks of St Petersburg. **Hernando de Soto** was the first European known to have set foot here (1539) – in search of gold; the area remained largely undeveloped for the next 200 years. First called Fort Brooke, the town became Tampa in 1855, named after the Indian word for 'sticks of fire'. Thirty years later, **Don Vicente Martinez Ybor** moved his cigar factory from Key West to Tampa, not only building a world-renowned industry here, but also forming the base of the city's thriving Hispanic community. Cubans followed the cigar maker in droves but the rising popularity of cigarettes brought a stop to an industry employing some 12,000 people. Today **Ybor City** remains one of the most vibrant areas of Tampa with excellent restaurants and lively nightlife as well as colourful markets.

The heart of the beautifully restored Ybor City is the former cigar factory, **Ybor Square**, which is now an attractive shopping mall with many speciality stores, antique shops and ethnic restaurants. The **Old Hyde Park Village** is another restored section of the city, and is filled with upmarket shops, pavement cafés and chic restaurants.

**West Coast**

**Left:** *Spanish and Cuban restaurants are a must in downtown Ybor City.*
**Below:** *Riding the Python at Busch Gardens is only for the brave.*

> **BUSCH GARDENS**
>
> Busch Gardens, north of downtown Tampa, has themed areas such as **Egypt**, where bazaars and entertainers abound. Explore King Tutankhamen's tomb, but don't miss Montu, the world's largest roller coaster with an inverted loop at 104ft (31m) and a peak G-force of 3.85. Other areas are the **Congo**, **Morocco**, **Nairobi**, **Serengeti Plain**, **Crown Colony**, **Stanleyville**, **Bird Gardens** and **Timbuktu**.

The skyscraper area downtown is home to the **Tampa Museum of Art** on N Ashley Drive. Seven galleries house Greek and Roman antiquities along with some of the finest exhibitions in the state. Dedicated to **African–American art**, the museum on N Marion Street was the first of its kind in Florida and is famed for its Barnett–Aden collection.

Children may prefer the **Museum of Science and Industry** (MOSI) on 4801 E Fowler Avenue. The planetarium, space simulators and hurricane chamber are both educational and fun. There's also the Butterfly Encounter (walk-through cages filled with butterflies) and an Omni Theater with a 360° revolving dome. Open 09:00–16:30 Sunday–Thursday in autumn and winter, 09:00–18:00 Sunday–Thursday and 09:00–21:00 Friday–Saturday in spring and summer.

Tampa has its share of theme parks, from **Adventure Island**, offering speed slides and other water attractions, to **Buccaneer Bay** with yet more sensational water rides in a natural spring setting.

The **Florida Aquarium** at Garrison Seaport Center covers 152,000ft$^2$ (14,121m$^2$) and houses 4350 species of fish, animal and plant, while **Lowry Park Zoo** on 7530 N Boulevard has a manatee treatment tank that doubles as an emergency rescue clinic.

## The Pinellas Peninsula ★★

A fist of land separating Tampa Bay from the Gulf of Mexico, the Pinellas Peninsula is largely consumed by uninteresting suburbia. However, the splendid coastline is fringed by a 28-mile (45km) string of barrier islands, locally called the Pinellas Suncoast, connected by road to the mainland and to each other by Gulf Boulevard. Adding to the obvious appeal of the beaches is the area's reputation for sunshine: 768 consecutive sunny days were recorded in the 1960s. Away from the coast, the area's only place of merit is the small city of St Petersburg.

## St Petersburg ★★

Once nationally-known as a retirement community, St Petersburg has enjoyed an influx of younger settlers and developed into a surprisingly vibrant and enjoyable place where most things of interest are within walking distance of one another. One major addition has been the **Florida International Museum** which turned a former department store into a vast exhibition space for major travelling shows. These have ranged from the treasures of the Russian Tsars to items recovered from the Titanic. Such is the museum's popularity, that bookings often have to be made in advance. Phone toll-free on 1-800 777 9882 for the latest exhibition and booking details.

A longer established but not less remarkable cultural offering is a major collection of works by the surrealist artist Salvador Dali. The **Salvador Dali Museum** was established by a wealthy American couple who befriended the artist on his first trip to the US in the 1930s and subsequently purchased many of his works. The museum is arranged to give a chronological view of Dali's work, from early orthodox paintings to the gigantic

**Below:** *Fabulous St Pete Beach, a good place to be on a hot day.*

canvases mostly created during the 1950s and '60s.

More curiosities are found beside the **Pier** where a 1960s **Russian submarine** can be toured as can, during the winter, the *Bounty*, the ship from the 1962 re-make of the film, *Mutiny on the Bounty*. The Pier itself is an enjoyable place to visit during the evening when free live music is offered on its upper level.

**The Pinellas Beaches** can be accessed by several routes across the peninsula. The most dramatic first impression, though, is found on the approach from St Petersburg on Route 682, with the bright pink profile of the **Don CeSar Hotel**, a luxury

Tampa Bay

resort, rising on the beach. Built in the 1920s, the Don CeSar (guided historical tours are available; tel: (727) 360 1881) marks the southern end of **St Pete Beach**, one of the biggest and busiest of the coastal communities. If time permits, head south into Pass-a-Grille, a village-like settlement with few trappings of tourism despite its excellent beaches and the enjoyably ramshackle **Gulf Beaches Historical Museum** on Tenth Avenue. Passing through St Pete Beach, the outlook of motels, restaurants and shopping plazas, and glimpses of uniformly excellent beaches, is one that continues for miles northwards on Gulf Boulevard. Worthwhile stops include Madeira Beach's **John's Pass Village** and the **Suncoast Seabird Sanctuary** (tel: (727) 391 6211) where injured birds are nursed back to health.

---

**TAMPA BAY HISTORY CENTER**

The glass-and-steel high rises of downtown Tampa do little to evoke the area's history but 12,000 years of local settlement are featured at the Tampa Bay History Center, at the corner of Franklin and Platt streets.

The exhibited maps, military uniforms, photos and artefacts reveal the area's rise from swampy outpost to thriving modern city. The center is open 10:00–17:00 Tuesday–Saturday, 13:00–17:00 Sunday; admission free.

**Above:** *The spotting of manatees is possible off Anna Maria Island's pier.* **Opposite:** *The impressive, well-kept grounds of the John and Mable Ringling Museum in Sarasota.*

**MANATEE SPOTTING**

Unfortunately the sea cow population is declining, but these gentle creatures still frequent the Gulf Coast. Good places to spot them include: **Terra Ceia Bay** at Sea Breeze Point; **Snead Island Emerson Point**; **Palma Sola Bay** on the Causeway and at Rose Park; **Manatee River**; Kingfish boat ramp, Coquina Beach Park, Leffis Key and Bayfront Park, all on **Anna Maria Island**. Sightings are guaranteed at the **South Florida Museum** in Bradenton.

## BRADENTON

The area was first inhabited by Timucuan Indians and, although visited by Spanish explorers, was not developed until 1842. Josiah Gates was the county's first permanent settler and **Major Robert Gamble** soon joined him. Gamble's house and huge plantation (the only surviving Antebellum plantation) can be visited on Patten Avenue in Bradenton. Open 09:00–17:00 Thursday–Monday. Guided tours 09:30, 10:30, 13:00–16:00 Thursday–Monday.

Set inland from the Gulf of Mexico, at the mouth of the Manatee River, Bradenton proudly preserves its historical roots. **Manatee Village Historical Park**, on Manatee Avenue takes visitors back in time with its carefully restored buildings. A memorial on 75th Street is dedicated to Hernando de Soto, the first Spaniard to land here, and the **South Florida Museum, Bishop Planetarium and Parker Manatee Aquarium** on 10th Street West covers the history of Florida from the Stone Age to the Space Age.

From Bradenton you can also enjoy a 75-minute ride aboard the **Florida Gulf Coast Railroad**. Alternatively, the world's largest airboat is available for trips through the **Myakka River State Park**, a dense woodland along the Myakka River and a breeding ground for numerous birds, which lies between Bradenton and Sarasota on Highway 72. Call ahead for opening times, tel: (941) 361-6511.

# SARASOTA

Sarasota considers itself the cultural capital of Florida, thanks in no small way to the influence of grand circus master **John Ringling** and his wife Mable. The city is home to the Florida West Coast Symphony and offers a marvellous host of artistic venues, such as the beautiful **Asolo Performing Arts Center** and the **Van Wezel Performing Arts Hall**.

The **Asolo Theater** is a 19th-century playhouse that was partly shipped from Asolo in Italy and was reconstructed in the United States. It is situated just up the road from **Bellm's Cars and Music of Yesterday**, which features an interesting collection of antique cars and more than 1500 musical antiques. Open 09:30–17:30 daily. The city's symphony orchestra performs regularly and there is a varied programme of fine opera and ballet productions. An annual jazz festival is held each April, as well as other community events such as the annual premier of the new circus season, dedicated to the memory of the famous Ringlings. Their Venetian-style winter home, **Ca'd'Zan**, which they designed after a visit to Europe, is open to the public and gives a taste of the wealth and glitz of the 1920s. Open 10:00–17:30 daily.

The adjacent **John and Mable Ringling Museum of Art** employs volunteer guides to take visitors around the 22-gallery maze of Old Masters and contemporary artworks, the classical courtyards adorned with statues, and Mable Ringling's fine rose garden. In honour of their circus background, the Ringlings also gave Sarasota the lovely **Circus Galleries** museum, housing gaily painted parade wagons, costumes and other circus memorabilia. Open 10:00–17:30 daily.

## BARRIER ISLANDS

**Egmont Key:** uninhabited island in Tampa Bay, with white, sandy beaches, a large population of turtles and excellent beachcombing. **Anna Maria Island:** a 7-mile (11km) island with a distinctly laid-back Caribbean feel. **Longboat Key:** tennis and golf are the main attractions on this upmarket island, which also holds the Mote Marine Aquarium and Pelican Man's Bird Sanctuary. **Lido and St Armands Keys:** resort area with glitzy shops and restaurants. **Siesta Key:** powdery sand and Point Rock, which is known for sponges, colourful shells and tropical fish.

**MARCO ISLAND**

Marco Island, 16 miles (26km) south of Naples, is the largest and only developed island of the Ten Thousand Island chain that runs down to the Florida Keys. Take a **trolley tour** to explore the island, dine out in one of the many excellent seafood restaurants or shop in the quaint old-style shopping centres. Indian burial mounds and a history of providing sanctuary for pirates gives the island plenty of folklore – and promise of buried treasure.

**Below:** *The Castaways Beach Plantation on Sanibel Island.*

## FORT MYERS

Fort Myers, developed during the Indian wars, started to grow in the late 1880s when tourists began to flock in.

### The Edison and Ford Homes ★★

Among the first arrivals was **Thomas Edison** who built a retreat on McGregor Boulevard. Adjacent to the house is a fascinating museum displaying hundreds of his inventions (some of the original light bulbs still burn). Tours only: 09:00–16:00 Monday–Saturday, noon–16:00 Sunday. Next door is Henry Ford's winter home, **Mangoes**. You can buy combination tickets to see both museums.

A few miles away is the **Fort Myers Historical Museum** with an interesting collection of Calusa Indian artefacts and Ethel Cooper glass. Parked outside is the *Esperanza*, longest and last of the Pullman coaches.

North of town lies the **Babcock Wilderness Adventure**, where you can join a 90-minute swamp-buggy tour and see bison, alligators, panthers, wild turkey and deer.

### Sanibel ★

Explore the **JN 'Ding' Darling National Wildlife Refuge**, where there is a five-mile (8km) drive alongside mangrove swamps as well as walkways, and cycling and canoe trails. Sanibel Island has five public beaches and the **Bailey-Matthews Shell Museum** (3075 Sanibel-Captiva Road), which holds about two million land and sea shells. Open 10:00–16:00 Tuesday–Sunday. Enthusiasts eager to collect their own may pick only dead shells on the beaches of Sanibel and Captiva. The best area is reputed to be the 'shell line', where the highest waves break on the beach. Please take note that a law introduced in 1995 strictly prohibits the gathering of live specimens.

## AROUND NAPLES

The city of Naples is really the main resort area of this wonderful stretch of the coast. It lies between the Gulf of Mexico and the Everglades, right at the northern tip of the **Ten Thousand Island** chain that runs down to the Florida Keys. Only **Marco Island** is developed.

### Naples *

Naples itself has little to offer in the way of museums or attractions, though the surrounding country has a wealth of places to explore. One exceptions in the city is the **Collier County Museum** which displays the history of the region from prehistoric to modern times.

**Above:** *Idyllic sands and sea in the Fort Myers area.*

The **Teddy Bear Museum** of Naples, on 2511 Pine Ridge Road, features a collection of more than 3000 lovable cuddly furry toys from around the world, displayed in a variety of novel poses.

The **Philharmonic Center for the Arts**, situated on Pelican Bay Boulevard, is the regional hub for the arts and music with four art galleries and two sculpture gardens, as well as a full yearly programme of events.

### Sanctuaries **

To explore the peaceful surrounding countryside, visit the **Conservancy's Naples Nature Center** on 1450 Merrihue Drive, where there are aquariums and a serpentarium. Boat tours are available from here. Or you can head 20 miles (32km) north of Naples to the **Corkscrew Swamp Sanctuary** where alligators, bobcats and otters live among giant bald cypress trees several hundreds of years old. The teeming birdlife will delight novices and ornithologists alike, and is best observed in winter when the birds tend to flock around the remaining pools of water.

---

**BARRIER ISLANDS**

**Boca Grande:** a retreat for the rich who enjoy its 19th-century atmosphere of wooden houses and sleepy fishing village.
**Cabbage Key:** a Calusa Indian shell mound lies under an inn built by playwright Mary Roberts Rinehart.
**Sanibel:** one-third of the island is dedicated to the **JN 'Ding' Darling National Wildlife Refuge**, named after a Pulitzer prize-winning cartoonist; shell-collecting here is exceptional.
**Gasparilla:** was once a favourite pirate haven.
**Captiva:** very popular among shell-seekers.

# The West Coast at a Glance

Locals pride themselves on the **360 days** of **sunshine** this region receives annually. Temperatures rarely fall below 60°F (15°C). In mid-summer 90°F (32°C) is common, but tempered by cool sea breezes. Near the **Everglades** it is rainy and humid in summer, with swarms of mosquitoes.

**Tampa International Airport** is rapidly expanding to cope with demand from Europe. It also has good United States connections. The **Sarasota–Bradenton International Airport** is well-serviced by American carriers. **Southwest Florida International Airport** serves the Fort Myers area and has expanded due to increased numbers of charters from Germany. **Car rental** companies are represented at convenient locations. Hotels operate airport **shuttle buses**. By car the West Coast is accessible off **Interstate 75** which runs north–south and from **Interstate 4** which heads west from Daytona Beach and Orlando. **Highway 19** hugs the coast from Tallahassee to St Petersburg. **Highway 41** runs down to Naples. From Miami the **Tamiami Trail** runs west to Naples. The **Everglades Parkway** connects Naples with Fort Lauderdale. **Greyhound:** good interstate service stops in Tampa, Sarasota, St Petersburg and Fort Myers.

**Road** networks are good and it is easy to cross the state to Orlando and the theme parks or down to the Everglades. The cities all have local **bus** networks. Clearwater Beach and Fort Myers Beach have **trolley services,** and **ferries** operate between the islands.

### Tampa
*LUXURY*
**Wyndham Harbour Island**, 725 S Harbour Island Blvd, tel: (813) 229-5000, fax: 229-5322. Rooms overlook the bay; walking distance to downtown.

*MID-RANGE*
**Holiday Inn Tampa Busch Gardens**, 2701 E Fowler Ave, tel: (813) 971-4710, fax: 979-0951. Close to theme park.

### St Petersburg
*LUXURY*
**Don CeSar Beach Resort**, 3400 Gulf Blvd, St Pete Beach, tel: (727) 360-1881, fax: 367-6952. Used by F Scott Fitzgerald and Al Capone.

*MID-RANGE*
**Howard Johnson Resort Hotel**, 6100 Gulf Blvd, tel: (727) 360-7041. 116-room hotel with beach access.

*BUDGET*
**Lamara Hotel Apartments**, 520 73rd Ave, tel: (727) 360-7521. Small hotel/motel with beach access and low rates.

### Clearwater area
*LUXURY*
**The Clearwater Beach Hotel**, 500 Mandalay Ave, tel: (727) 441-2425, www.clearwater-beachhotel.com Overlooks Gulf of Mexico; private beach.

*MID-RANGE*
**Best Western Sea Wake Inn**, 691 S Gulfview Blvd, Clearwater Beach, tel: (727) 443-7652, fax: 461-2836. On the beach.

*BUDGET*
**Chart House Suites**, 850 Bay Way Blvd, Clearwater Beach, tel: (727) 449-8007, fax: 443-6081. Overlooks the bay.

### Sarasota area
*LUXURY*
**Hyatt Sarasota**, 1000 Blvd of the Arts, tel: (941) 953-1234, fax: 952-1987. In city centre; some rooms overlook bay area.

*MID-RANGE*
**The Helmsley Sandcastle Hotel**, 1540 Ben Franklin Drive, tel: (941) 388-2181, fax: 388-2655. Beside beach on Lido Key.

### Naples
*LUXURY*
**La Playa Beach Resort**, 9891 Gulf Shore Drive, tel: (239) 597-3123, www.laplayaresort.com Targets golfers and honeymooners; sunset-view rooms.
**The Registry Resort**, 475 Seagate Drive, tel: (239) 597-3232, www.registryresort.com Luxury resort; has shuttle through mangroves to beach.

# The West Coast at a Glance

*MID-RANGE*
**Vanderbilt Beach Resort**,
9225 Gulfshore Drive, tel:
(239) 597-3144, www.
vanderbiltbeachresort.com
Beachfront motel with dock
and boat ramp.

*BUDGET*
**Inn at Pelican Bay**, 800
Vanderbilt Beach Rd, tel:
(239) 597-8777, www.
innatpelicanbay.com  Small
hotel with European style.

## WHERE TO EAT

*Tampa*
**Columbia Restaurant**, 2117 E
7th Ave, Ybor City, tel: (813)
248-4961. Claims to be America's oldest Spanish restaurant.
**Ceviche Restaurant & Tapas
Bar**, 2109 Bayshore Blvd, tel:
(813) 250-0203. Serving
Spanish cuisine nightly.

*St Petersburg*
**Hurricane**, 9th Ave and Gulf
Way, tel: (727) 360-9558. Very
casual, excellent seafood.
**Wine Cellar**, 17307 Gulf Blvd,
N Redington Beach, tel: (727)
393-3491. International menu,
highly acclaimed.

*Clearwater*
**Bascom's Chop House**, 3665
Ulmerton Rd, Clearwater, tel:
(727) 573-3363. American
cuisine; smart, with dress code.
Reservations recommended.
**Hogfish Grill**, 1800 Gulf to
Bay Blvd, tel: (727) 446-7027,
New eaterie winning accolades
for its barbeque seafood.

*Sarasota area*
**Columbia Restaurant**, 411 St
Armands Circle, tel: (941) 388-
3987. Reservations required;
long-standing reputation for
Spanish/Cuban cuisine.
**Marina Jack**, 2 Marina Plaza,
tel: (941) 365-4232. Outdoor
waterfront dining in downtown area, children welcome.
Good value during the day,
more expensive in the evening.

*Naples*
**Dock Restaurant**, 845 12th
Ave S., tel: (239) 263-9940,
Waterfront dining, happy hour,
children welcome, gift shop.
**Ridgway Bar & Grill**, 1300
Third St, S., tel: (239) 262-
5500. Open all day; classic
American; children welcome;
reservations recommended.

## SHOPPING

**Centro Ybor**, 1600 E 8th St,
Tampa, tel: (813) 242-4660.
Excellent shopping, dining and
entertainment in the centre of
the historic area.
**International Plaza & Bay St**,
2223 N Westshore Blvd,
Tampa, tel: (813) 342-3790.
Courtesy shuttle to this mall
near airport; almost 200 stores.

**Prime Outlets at Naples**,
6060 Collier Blvd, Naples, tel:
(239) 775-8083, manufacturers'
outlet mall; discounted prices.

## TOURS AND EXCURSIONS

**Around The Bend Nature
Tours**, 1815 Palma Sola Blvd,
Bradenton, tel: (941) 794-
8773, www.aroundbend.com
Nature walks and boat tours.
**Skydive City**, 4241 SkyDive
Ln, Zephyrhills, tel: (813) 783-
9399, www.skydivecity.com
**Baseball** spring training
camps; Tampa Bay
Buccaneers offer NFL games.

## USEFUL CONTACTS

**Convention and Visitors
Bureau Information Centers:**
**Tampa Bay**, 615 Channelside
Dr, tel: (813) 223-2752,
www.VisitTampaBay.com
**St Petersburg/Clearwater
Area**, 14450–46th St, Suite
108, Clearwater, tel: (727)
464-7200, www.
floridasbeach.com
**Bradenton Area**, One Haben
Blvd, Palmetto tel: (941) 729-
9177, www.flagulfislands.com
**Sarasota**, 655 N Tamiami
Trail, tel: 0800 522 9799,
www.sarasotafl.org

| TAMPA | J | F | M | A | M | J | J | A | S | O | N | D |
|---|---|---|---|---|---|---|---|---|---|---|---|---|
| AVERAGE TEMP. °F | 60 | 62 | 66 | 71 | 77 | 81 | 82 | 82 | 81 | 75 | 68 | 62 |
| AVERAGE TEMP. °C | 16 | 17 | 19 | 22 | 25 | 27 | 28 | 28 | 27 | 24 | 20 | 17 |
| HOURS OF SUN DAILY | 12 | 12 | 12 | 13 | 13 | 14 | 14 | 14 | 13 | 12 | 12 | 12 |
| RAINFALL in | 2 | 3 | 3 | 1 | 3 | 5 | 7 | 8 | 6 | 2 | 2 | 2 |
| RAINFALL mm | 51 | 76 | 76 | 25 | 76 | 127 | 178 | 203 | 152 | 51 | 51 | 51 |
| DAYS OF RAINFALL | 7 | 8 | 8 | 7 | 9 | 13 | 14 | 12 | 11 | 9 | 7 | 7 |

# 8
# The Florida Keys

The Florida Keys and Key West, to give the area its correct name, is an approximately 180-mile (290km) chain of islands trailing off Florida's southeastern tip and arcing to the southwest into the Atlantic. The northernmost island of **Key Largo** is the land base for the **John Pennekamp Coral Reef State Park**. The most southerly point, the **Dry Tortugas**, lies just about 85 miles (137km) north of Havana, Cuba.

An official count for the number of islands is unavailable, but estimates put the total at around 800, spread over 2700 sq miles (6995km²) of coral reefs. Forty-two of the islands are linked by the 113 mile (182km) US1, or **Overseas Highway**, which spans 43 bridges including the famous **Seven Mile Bridge**.

Despite the road link, most of the islands are accessible only by water. This has ensured that the region is able to preserve a feeling of the past; today all the islands are protected by the **Florida Keys National Marine Sanctuary**. Fishing, sunning and snorkelling are still the main activities and nightlife is limited to eating out and sampling the different bars. The atmosphere is unlike that in any other part of Florida – this could easily be the Caribbean, rather than the United States.

One of this region's most famous residents, author **Ernest Hemingway**, has come to epitomize the lifestyle of the Keys, and little has changed since he lived, wrote and fished here – except for the growing number of visitors who head south to try and capture the spirit of these beguiling, laid-back islands.

**DON'T MISS**

**\*\*\* The Dolphin Research Center, Grassy Key:** inspired the popular movie *Flipper*.
**\*\* The Wrecker's Museum, Key West:** pirate mementos, and marine artefacts.
**\*\* Mallory Square, Key West:** admire the sunset.
**\*\* John Pennekamp State Park, Key Largo:** first underwater state park; America's only living coral reef.
**\* *African Queen*, Key Largo:** original boat used by Humphrey Bogart and Katharine Hepburn in the movie *African Queen*.

**Opposite:** *Underwater adventures abound in the Florida Keys.*

## KEY LARGO

The largest island in the chain at nearly 30 miles (48km) long, Key Largo is also the most developed. Key Largo claims to be the **diving capital** of the USA and, while this title might be disputed by some, there's no doubt the place is popular with divers. The **John Pennekamp Coral Reef State Park** was the first underwater sanctuary in America, established in order to protect part of the only living coral reef in the United States. It covers 53,661 acres (21,716ha) of submerged land and 2350 acres (951ha) above water. Visitors can enjoy a full range of water sports and sightseeing activities. The wonderland of 500 species of fish and 55 varieties of coral is also accessible to non-swimmers via glass-bottom boats.

Land-based attractions include the **Crocodile Lakes National Wildlife Refuge** and the original *African Queen* steamboat, which featured in a film starring Humphrey Bogart and Katharine Hepburn. The boat has been fully restored and now rests at the Key Largo Harbor Marina. There's also the 1951 Chris-Craft, used as a prop in the film *On Golden Pond*, again starring Katharine Hepburn alongside veteran actor Henry Fonda.

In historical Tavernier, the station, churches and pioneer homes date back to the turn of the century.

### CLIMATE

Winter (December–April) lows average 65°–70°F (18°–21°C). **Summer** (July–October) is **hot** and **humid** with highs around 90°F (32°C). **Hurricane season** is from **August–October** with storms most likely in late August and September.

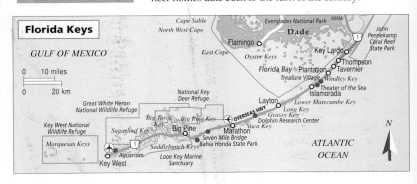

## THE UPPER KEYS
### Windley Key **

After passing through **Plantation Key**, named for its many tropical fruit farms, you reach **Windley Key** and the **Theater of the Sea**. Here you can see dolphins, even swim alongside them (by prior appointment, for the over-13s, and only after a 30-minute orientation crash course), or meet a live shark. There is a 'bottomless' boat to ride, as well as entertaining dolphin and sea lion shows. A new attraction is the **Trainer for a Day** pro-gramme which includes three hours of caring for and feeding the dolphins, with lessons on anatomy, physiol-ogy and dolphin behaviour. Open 09:30–16:00 daily.

The **Hurricane Memorial** at MM82 (Mile Marker 82) marks the mass grave of 423 construction workers who lost their lives during the 1935 Labor Day hurricane. **Windley Key Fossil Reef Geological Site** at MM85.3 offers free tours of a 30-acre (12ha) area of pristine hum-mocks, fauna and archaeological sites.

### Islamorada *

Billed as the **sport fishing capital** of the world, this is the perfect base for deep-sea fishing expeditions. Marlin, tuna and dolphin (a fish – also called *mahi-mahi* – and not the mammal) are found just offshore in the Atlantic, while tarpon and bonefish offer shallow-water challenges.

Admiring without catching is possible thanks to numerous dive and snorkel charters on the island. At **Treasure Village,** on Old Highway, you can examine salvaged treasures and browse through shops and galleries. South of Isla-morada lies Long Key and the lovely **Long Key State Recreation Area**, a place to relax, fish, swim, go canoe-ing or walking. Book ahead for the camping facilities, particularly in peak season.

> **DIVING SURPRISES**
>
> The Keys are famed for their excellent scuba diving within a few miles of the shore and for a few odd underwater surprises:
> • The 10ft (3m) **Christ of the Deep** statue is submerged in 25ft (8m) of water and sur-rounded by a wealth of coral fish. It was a gift to the Under-water Society of America from an Italian dive equipment manufacturer and is a smaller copy of the Christ of the Abysses that lies submerged off the town of Genoa in Italy.
> • The **Jules Undersea Lodge** houses guests in a lodge 30ft (9m) underwater. It is hugely popular – book at least a year in advance.
> • The **Spiegel Grove**, a 510ft (155m) navy ship, was inten-tionally scuttled in 2002 as the backbone for a new coral reef.

**Opposite:** *The Christ of the Deep, 25ft (8m) under-water at John Pennekamp Coral Reef State Park.*
**Below:** *Idyllic island life on Upper Matecumbe Key.*

Just offshore from Islamorada lies **Lignumvitae Key**, a 280-acre (113ha) tropical relic of centuries gone by. Scientists estimate that some of the flora dates back more than 10,000 years. They named the island after the *lignum vitae* (wood of life) trees found here.

The island was bought by chemist William Matheson in 1919, but apart from a house, a small clearing and a dock, he left nature untouched. Bought by the state in 1972, the island is now open to the public for guided **tours** only, but closed every Tuesday and Wednesday.

Nearby, at the **San Pedro Underwater Archaeological Preserve**, lies the 287-ton Dutch-built *San Pedro* which sank in 1733. Rediscovered in 1960 in 18ft (5½m) of water, much of the wreck was hauled back to the surface. Today it is a very popular dive site with a pile of ballast stones to mark the spot, as well as replica cannons, an anchor and an underwater information plate.

## Marathon *

Before reaching Marathon, at MM59 on Grassy Key is the **Dolphin Research Center**, which works with universities and research facilities around the world. Here too, you can swim with the dolphins but need to book well ahead (at least a month before your intended visit). This was once the site of Flipper's Sea School for training dolphins and here the original 1950s *Flipper* movie was filmed.

Marathon itself has an excellent natural history museum, and the **Crane Point Hammock**, an archaeological

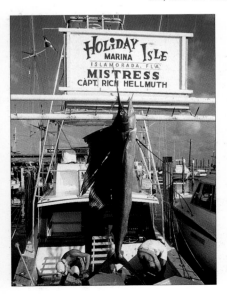

site with finds dating back some seven centuries, and the oldest example of Conch-style architecture outside of Key West. Short walking trails from the museum weave through the tropical forest that holds the historic sites.

Driving south from Marathon, you cross the famous **Seven Mile Bridge** which actually measures only 6.9 miles (11km). It was completed in 1982 at a cost of US$45 million and is the world's longest segmental bridge. Every April, runners gather in Marathon for a special bridge race. At MM47 lies the pedestrian entrance to the **Old Seven Mile Bridge**. The structure is listed on the National Register of Historic Places and, across the Middle to Lower Keys, it rests on 546 concrete pillars.

## THE LOWER KEYS

The area from Seven Mile Bridge south to Key West is known as the **Lower Keys**. This is what people dream of when they think of the Keys: peace and quiet, stunning views and undisturbed wildlife. Parks include the **Bahia Honda State Park** with cabins and camp sites overlooking the ocean, the **Looe Key National Marine**

Sanctuary named after the HMS *Looe* which ran aground here in 1744, and the **National Key Deer Refuge**, which is home to several hundred miniature deer. A subspecies of the Virginia white-tailed deer, this little animal has been under threat from encroaching human development and traffic on the main highway.

**Above:** *The strange Ripley's Believe It or Not! in Duval Street, Key West.*
**Opposite:** *Catch of the day – a huge marlin caught off the Florida Keys.*

### Key West ★★★

Key West has become a legend in its own lifetime, a place people visit to experience something different. Once a barely accessible paradise for escapists, Key West has since been forced into the mainstream by hordes of tourists yet retains some of the quirkiness that makes it so unique.

In April 1982 the United States Border Patrol set up roadblocks across the Overseas Highway just south of Florida City in an attempt to stem the flow of illegal aliens from here into the United States. Traffic chaos ensued as police searched every vehicle, demanding occupants produce proof of their US citizenship. In protest at being treated like foreigners in their own country, city officials of Key West proclaimed the **Conch Republic**, complete with separate flag, mock visas, border passes and currency, forcing a chagrined border patrol to beat a hasty retreat. 'Conch' passports and visas are still available from the Key West Chamber of Commerce and the Conch Republic Celebration, in honour of the 'secessionists victory', is held in April every year.

Always out on a limb, the Key West inhabitants started out as **wreckers**, aiding the victims of shipwrecks and rescuing cargo, though stories of deliberate wrecking abound.

Its uniqueness has subsequently appealed to eccentrics and celebrities. The committed environmentalist **John Audubon** started preservation awareness and helped retain much of the history of the island. **Ernest Hemingway** found inspiration for much of his work while living here.

Key West is hedonism at its best. In the evening, head down **Duval Street** to festive **Mallory Square**, where locals and tourists mingle with jugglers, fire eaters and buskers, as the sun sets to a round of applause. Mallory Square forms the starting point for lively evenings out in the many bars, cafés and restaurants, most of which have excellent live music with a Caribbean flavour.

During the day, a good place to start a tour is on Truman Avenue. Turn left on Lean Street to find the home of playwright **Tennessee Williams**. Continue down

---

**END OF THE ROAD**

The cluster of islands lying beyond Key West is called the **Dry Tortugas**. Known as the Gibraltar of the Gulf due to their strategic position, they were of prime military importance in the past. Fort Jefferson on Garden Key has artillery tiers for 450 guns and 50ft (15m) walls 8ft (2½m) thick. Used as a prison after the Civil War, it is now a tourist site.

---

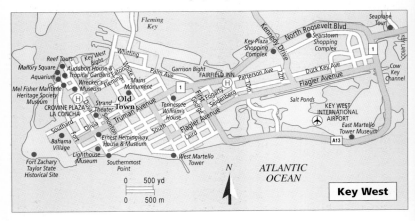

Key West

Truman Avenue and turn left into **Whitehead Street** to reach the most southerly point of mainland America accessible to the public. Turn right to find the **Lighthouse Museum** where you can climb 98 steps for lovely views across the island and out to sea.

Almost opposite is the unusual **Hemingway House** (open 09:00–17:00 daily). Dating back to 1851, this was the famous author's home from 1931 to 1940. It was the first house in Key West to have running water, a fireplace and a pool. The headboard of the bed is made from a 17th-century Spanish monastery gate, the glass chandelier was hand-blown and the Picasso cat was a gift to the author from Pablo Picasso himself. The house is now a museum and inhabited by 42 cats (most with six toes or more), one for each bridge in the Keys.

Left off Whitehead and into Petronia Street, you reach the lively Caribbean-style **Bahama Village** neighbourhood. Further north, at the corner of Whitehead Street and **Greene Street**, among a row of irresistibly quaint 'gingerbread' conch-style houses, is the **Audubon House**, filled with a priceless collection of furniture from the mid-1800s and original bird engravings by the artist. Open 09:30–17:00 daily.

Opposite is the **Mel Fisher Maritime Heritage Society Museum**, housing treasure that was lost by two Spanish galleons which foundered during a hurricane in 1622. Just down the road, back on Duval Street, is the **Wrecker's Museum**, built in 1829 for Florida Senator Watlington, who was also a sea captain and wrecker. The house is said to be the oldest in Key West.

The delightful pink and green house at the end of the street is often called the Southernmost House. This is actually a misnomer, since another one was erected just south of it.

**HEMINGWAY DAYS**

Ernest 'Papa' Hemingway wrote *For Whom the Bell Tolls*, *The Green Hills of Africa*, *The Snows of Kilimanjaro*, *Death in the Afternoon* and *The Old Man and the Sea* while living on Whitehead Street in Key West, between organizing boxing matches and drinking at Sloppy Joe's.

**Opposite:** *Famous author, Ernest Hemingway, accessed his study via a catwalk.*
**Below:** *Aerial view of Fort Jefferson (Dry Tortugas).*

# The Florida Keys at a Glance

## BEST TIMES TO VISIT

The climate is kinder in the Keys than on the mainland. **Summer** temperatures reach 80°F (27°C) in July and drop to around 70°F (21°C) in the winter. Winds keep the islands **free of humidity** in summer and warm in winter. **Hurricane** season extends from **August** to **October** and tropical storms occur throughout the summer months. The Keys are busy in winter, but limited accommodation keeps tourist numbers to manageable levels.

## GETTING THERE

**Key West International Airport** is on the southeast corner of the island, while **Marathon Airport** is on Marathon at MM52. Direct international flights into the Keys are not available and most visitors use Miami as a gateway – flying time is 45 minutes to Key West and 35 minutes to Marathon. The majority of visitors arrive by car. The only road to the Keys is **Highway 1** (the Overseas Highway), which heads south out of Florida City and continues down to Key West across 43 bridges. This road is marked per mile, directions are given by **Mile Marker** (MM) with MM1 on the tip of Key West. There is no train service, since the line was destroyed by a hurricane in the 1930s, but you can arrive by yacht or cruise line.

## GETTING AROUND

Most of the islands are small enough to explore on foot, but taxis are available. Key West has two tourist services, known as:
**Conch Tour Train**,
tel: (305) 294-5161
and **Old Town Trolley**,
1910 N Roosevelt Blvd,
tel: (305) 296-6688.
Both of these take about 90 minutes to tour the town.

## WHERE TO STAY

You should book ahead for any establishment in the Keys. The relatively few hotels are extremely popular, particularly around Christmas, in the summer season and on United States holiday weekends.

### Key Largo
*LUXURY*
**Holiday Inn Key Largo Resort and Marina**, 99701 Overseas Highway, tel: (305) 451-2121, fax: 451-5592. Renovated by the man who also restored the *African Queen*, moored outside.
**Marriott Key Largo Bay Beach Resort**, 103800 Overseas Highway, tel (305) 453-0000. Luxurious resort on the beach.

*MID-RANGE*
**Marina del Mar Resort and Marina**, 527 Caribbean Drive, Key Largo, tel: (305) 451-4107, fax: 451-1891.Offers a deepwater marina; with some of the world's best diving nearby.

**Ocean Point Suites**,
500 Burton Drive, Key Largo,
tel: (305) 853-3000.

### Islamorada
*LUXURY*
**Checca Lodge**, MM82, Upper Matecumbe Key, tel: (305) 664-4651, fax: 664-2893. Won awards for its environmentally friendly schemes. Calm and spacious.

*MID-RANGE*
**Casa Morada**, 136 Madeira Road, tel: (305) 664-0044.
**Pelican Cove**, 84457 Old Overseas Highway, tel: (305) 664-4435.

### Duck Key
*LUXURY*
**Hawk's Cay Resort**,
tel: (305) 743-7000.
With dolphin experience.
**Faro Blanco Marine Resort**,
tel: (305) 743-9018.

*MID-RANGE*
**Banana Bay Resort and Marina**, 4590 Overseas Highway, tel: (305) 743-3500, fax: 743-2670. A beautiful and very relaxing resort.
**Sombero Resort and Lighthouse Marina**, 19 Sombero Beach Blvd, tel: (305) 743-2250, fax: 743-2998. Suites all have kitchens, good marina.

*BUDGET*
**Seascape Oceanfront Resort**, tel: (305) 743-6455.
**Howard Johnson Resort**, tel: toll free (800) 321-3496.

# The Florida Keys at a Glance

## Key West
### LUXURY
**The Banyan Resort**, 323 Whitehead St, tel: (305) 296-7786, fax: 294-1107. Within walking distance of Old Town attractions; pleasant gardens.
**Crowne Plaza La Concha**, 430 Duval St, tel: (305) 296-2991, fax: 294-3283. Seven storeys of Art Deco; guests have included Ernest Hemingway and Tennessee Williams.
**Fairfield Inn**, 2400 N Roosevelt Blvd, tel: (305) 296-5700, fax: 292-9840. Free breakfast, two pools and only a mile from downtown.

### WHERE TO EAT

The Keys have their very own cuisine with an emphasis on seafood. Eat stone crabs in season (15 Oct–15 May), when they can legally be harvested. Definitely sample Key lime pie.

### Key Largo
**Mrs Mac's Kitchen**, MM99, tel: (305) 451-3722. Very good food; lovely international decor.

### Islamorada
**Marker 88 Restaurant**, tel: (305) 852-9315. Casual but costly, award-winning food in a tropical setting.

### Marathon
**Grassy Key Dairy Bar**, MM58.5, tel: (305) 743-3816. Good food at good prices.
**Kelsey's**, M48, 1996 Overseas Highway, Docks of Faro Blanco Resort, tel: (305) 743-9018.

Beautiful setting, overlooking ocean; local dishes a speciality.

### Key West
**Pepe's Cafe and Steak House**, 806 Caroline St, tel: (305) 294-7192. Best place in town for breakfast; meet locals in this small shack which serves affordable meals all day long.
**Half Shell Raw Bar**, Land's End Marina, tel: (305) 294-7496. Huge plates of oysters and conch chowder are two of the best dishes.
**Sloppy Joe's**, 201 Duval St, tel: (305) 294-8585. Former haunt of Ernest Hemingway, now a tourist trap but still a definite 'must see'.

### SHOPPING

Not much exciting shopping is to be had in the Keys, beyond the normal resort shops, and souvenir T-shirt stalls.
**Mallory Square**, Key West, tel: (305) 296-4557. Main centre, .
**The Rain Barrel**, Islamorada. Art show in March with 100 artists and some 20,000 visitors.
**Fast Buck Freddie's**, 500 Duval St. A Greenpeace outpost selling rather offbeat items like Pelican Poop.

### TOURS AND EXCURSIONS

**Yankee Freedom II Dry Tortugas National Park Ferry**, 240 Margaret St, Key West, tel: (305) 294-7009. Cruise on a 100ft catamaran to Fort Jefferson and the Dry Tortugas.
**Old Town Trolley Tours**, Mallory Square, Key West, tel: (305) 296-6688. 90-minute tour of attractions with 12 stops along the way.
**Conch Tour Train**, 501 Front St, Key West, tel: (305) 294-5161. 90-minute tours.

### USEFUL CONTACTS

**Florida Keys and Key West Development Council**, 1201 White St, tel: (305) 296-1552, web: www.fla-keys.com
**Key West Information Center**, 1601 N Roosevelt Blvd, Key West, tel: (305) 292-5000, web: www.keywestinfo.com
**Key Largo Chamber of Commerce/Florida Keys Visitor Center**, 106000 Overseas Hwy, Key Largo, tel: (305) 451-1414, web: www. keylargochamber.org
**Coast Guard Group Key West**, tel: (305) 292-8727. Information on navigational hazards, safety and weather.

| KEY WEST | J | F | M | A | M | J | J | A | S | O | N | D |
|---|---|---|---|---|---|---|---|---|---|---|---|---|
| AVERAGE TEMP. °F | 65 | 67 | 68 | 72 | 74 | 77 | 79 | 79 | 77 | 76 | 70 | 67 |
| AVERAGE TEMP. °C | 18 | 19 | 20 | 22 | 23 | 25 | 26 | 26 | 25 | 24 | 21 | 19 |
| HOURS OF SUN DAILY | 12 | 12 | 12 | 13 | 13 | 14 | 14 | 14 | 13 | 12 | 12 | 12 |
| RAINFALL in | 2 | 2 | 2 | 3 | 6.5 | 9 | 6 | 7 | 8 | 7 | 2.5 | 2 |
| RAINFALL mm | 51 | 51 | 51 | 76 | 165 | 229 | 152 | 179 | 203 | 179 | 63 | 51 |
| DAYS OF RAINFALL | 7 | 7 | 7 | 8 | 12 | 15 | 13 | 13 | 14 | 13 | 8 | 7 |

# Travel Tips

## Tourist Information

The Florida Commission on Tourism (represented as Visit Florida) has branches in London, Paris, Toronto and in South America. The **London** office receives personal callers by prior appointment only, tel: 020 7932 2406. For a free Florida information pack tel: 01737 644882.The head office is in **Tallahassee**, Suite 30D, 661 East Jefferson St, tel: (850) 488-5607, web: www.FLAUSA.com  Each county and city has its own separate tourism office. Greater **Miami** Convention and Visitors Bureau, tel: (305) 539-3000, web: www. miamiandbeaches.com Greater **Fort Lauderdale** Convention and Visitors Bureau, tel: (954) 765-4466, web: www.sunny.org **Tampa Bay** Convention and Visitors Bureau, tel: (813) 223-2752, web: www. VisitTampaBay.com **St Petersburg–Clearwater** Area Convention and Visitors Bureau, tel: (727) 464-7200, web: www.floridasbeach.com **Orlando–Orange County** Convention and Visitors Bureau, tel: (407) 363-5872, web: www.orlandoinfo.com **Kissimmee–St Cloud** Convention and Visitors **Bureau**, tel: (407) 847-5000, web: www.floridakiss.com **Daytona Beach Area** Convention and Visitors Bureau, tel: (386) 255-0415, web: www.daytonabeach.com **Jacksonville and the Beaches** Convention and Visitors Bureau, tel: (904) 798-9111, web: www.visitjacksonville.com Information about attractions can be obtained from **Florida Attractions Association**, Box 10295, Tallahassee FL32302, tel: (850) 222-2885. Information about state parks and recreation areas comes from **Office of Recreation and Parks**, Mail Station 535, 3900 Commonwealth Blvd, Tallahassee, FL32399-3000, tel: (850) 488-9872.

## Entry Requirements

Since 9/11, security systems have been tightened. Visitors should **check the latest rules before travelling** but, at the time of print, visitors must be in possession of a valid machine readable passport and be able to show a return air ticket. EU citizens may enter the US under the visa waiver scheme and will be given the necessary forms as they enter the country. Anyone on a fly-drive vacation must have an address for the first night. All children now need to travel on their own passport. Anyone staying longer than 90 days must have a visa. Citizens other than those from Britain, New Zealand, Japan and most western European countries need a valid passport that expires at least six months after their visit to the US has ended. Multiple re-entry visas are valid for 10 years and can be transferred to new passports. Visa costs vary according to nationality. Those with multiple re-entry visas will be able to enter blue lanes at immigration points, which should be quicker.
In Britain, visas can be obtained in writing from the **Visa and Immigration Dept of the United States**, United States Embassy, 5 Upper Grosvenor St, London W1A 2JB, tel: (020 7) 499-3443.

## Customs

Customs forms have to be completed before arrival. Familiar red and green channels greet visitors at the airport. Allowances for non-resident adults (over 21) are: 1 litre spirits, 200 cigarettes or 50 cigars or 2kg of tobacco, and 100ml of perfume. Unlicensed importation of fruit, plants and meat is banned – travel snacks like apples will be confiscated.

## Health Requirements

No vaccinations are required to enter the US, unless coming from an area suffering from outbreaks of cholera or yellow fever. However, adequate health insurance cover is essential. Florida has a very good health and dental care system but it is extremely expensive. Carry a doctor's prescription to allay fears of drug smuggling if you are on medication involving narcotics or syringes.

## Getting There

**By Air:** All main US carriers fly into Florida. The major gateways from Europe are Miami International Airport and Orlando International Airport, although an increasing amount of traffic is handled by Tampa. St Petersburg and Sanford international airports receive charter flights from Europe. All the bigger cities have regional airports with extensive connections from the main entry points into Florida and from other parts of the United States.

**By Road:** The network of

the efficient Greyhound bus service extends all over the United States and into Florida.

**By Rail:** Amtrak operates a national service, though few areas in Florida are connected. The main railway line runs down to Miami but bypasses some of the central east coast. There are no links through the Everglades or into the Keys.

**By Boat:** With so many thousands of kilometres of coastline, Florida has a large variety of ports, marinas and docks. Most major cruise lines regularly dock in a Florida port, and yacht charters are available to and from the region. An abundance of ferry services operate from mainland destinations to the offshore barrier islands.

## What to Pack

Florida, generally, is very casual. Pack according to season. Take a jumper in winter, particularly if visiting the north of the state. In summer, pack light, loose clothing for humid weather and be prepared for tropical rainstorms. You'll need plenty of sun cream and don't forget sunglasses and a hat. Comfortable shoes are a necessity for theme parks, which usually require a lot of walking and queueing. In summer, mosquitoes and other biting bugs are rampant, so take enough repellent. Don't worry if you do forget something; it will be available across the state, probably at less cost than at home.

## Money Matters

**Currency:** The official currency is the dollar, symbolized by the $ sign. One dollar is divided into 100 cents in the following denominations: 5 cents (nickel), 10 cents (dime) and 25 cents (quarter). Avoid carrying large sums in cash with you and ideally use US currency traveller's cheques. Note that cheques in pound sterling and other European currencies will not be changed except at the bigger banks. Major credit cards are widely accepted and most Americans use plastic rather than cash.

**Exchange:** Foreign exchange desks are located at airports and a few large banks and hotels. Banks are generally open 10:00–15:00 Mon–Thu, and 10:00–17:00 Fri. Hotels and car hire companies may require a credit card swipe before handing over a vehicle or checking you in.

**Tipping:** Most restaurants and bars add a 15% service charge to your bill, but an additional tip is expected for good service. Taxi drivers expect at least 10% in tips, and airport and hotel porters demand a minimum of US$1 per bag.

**Sales tax:** The six per cent is not usually included in the displayed price, and will be added to the bill at the check out.

## Accommodation

Florida offers an enormous choice of accommodation. Peak season varies from north to south but, generally speaking, if you plan to be in the south in winter or in the north in summer, book ahead. Accommodation varies from inexpensive motels to high-rise tourist hotels. Luxury resorts are often low-rise and spread over hundreds of acres. City-centre hotels and those near the major airports tend to cater for business travellers and are priced accordingly. All the major American hotel chains are well represented in the state and will book you into other chain members elsewhere on request.

Note: the rate is usually for the room, not per person. Most reservations are kept until 17:00 or 18:00, but this can be extended if the hotel is warned in advance of your late arrival. Most establishments will require at least one night's payment in advance, or a tour operator voucher or proof of payment.

Do not commit yourself unnecessarily to half-board or even bed and breakfast – eating out is so cheap, that many hotels quote a simple room rate knowing guests prefer to eat elsewhere.

## Eating Out

Florida prides itself on its fresh seafood and freshly grown fruits and vegetables. Portions are large and prices generally low. Meals can be true feasts, with pancakes and massive omelettes for breakfast, and eat-as-much-as-you-can buffets in the evening. On Sunday, breakfast and lunch will often be merged into brunch, a massive banquet, frequently served with a glass of champagne, orange juice or a Bloody Mary.

It is interesting to note the regional differences within the state. To the north the food is influenced by Southern cooking and Creole cuisine. Grits, okra (a long, thin vegetable), fried aubergine (eggplant), fried chicken and corn bread are among the staples. Further south the cooking is influenced by 20th-century immigrants. Spicy Cuban and Caribbean foods are commonplace in Miami, where Spanish style also abounds. Alligator appears on menus seasonally: try it, it tastes a bit like chicken, and is reassuringly eco-friendly, coming from a well-orchestrated culling programme. In the Keys, the food is slightly different again – there is much more delectable seafood and, of course, tasty Key lime pie for dessert.

## Transport

**Air:** All major US carriers fly into Florida, while American Eagle, Delta and USAir offer comprehensive networks within Florida. The air passes of some airlines cost much the same as bus or rail tickets – a good bargain.

**Road:** Road networks are good, with major and interstate highways (motorways) running north to south and east to west. There are a few toll roads. Most towns and cities are laid out on a grid system, many based on numbered streets, which usually run in one direction only, with avenues or boulevards intersecting at 90-degree angles. All car rental companies have outlets in the major centres

| CONVERSION CHART | | |
|---|---|---|
| FROM | TO | MULTIPLY BY |
| Millimetres | Inches | 0.0394 |
| Metres | Yards | 1.0936 |
| Metres | Feet | 3.281 |
| Kilometres | Miles | 0.6214 |
| Kilometres square | Square miles | 0.386 |
| Hectares | Acres | 2.471 |
| Litres | Pints | 1.760 |
| Kilograms | Pounds | 2.205 |
| Tonnes | Tons | 0.984 |
| To convert Celsius to Fahrenheit: x 9 ÷ 5 + 32 | | |

and at airports – shop around for the best deal. Fly-drive packages often present the cheapest and easiest way of arranging a car. Anyone over 16, with a valid driving licence, can drive in Florida, though most rental companies insist that drivers be over 25. Insurance may be arranged by the car hire firm.

**Road Rules:** Driving is on the right. Rectangular green road signs usually provide directions, while yellow signs contain safety information. White signs show speed limits: 15mph (24kph) in school zones, 25mph (40kph) on residential streets and between 35–55mph (56–88kph) on main streets. Interstate highways are usually 55mph (90kph) in towns and 65mph (105kph) in rural areas. All front-seat passengers must wear seat belts. Children under three must sit in approved car seats, which rental companies can usually supply. You should drive with headlights on if it rains hard enough to have to use windshield wipers. Florida's anti-drink-drive laws are tough: offenders face heavy fines and possible jail terms. If you park unlawfully or overstay your metered time, your vehicle will be towed away. Parking within three metres of a fire hydrant is an offence. It is illegal to leave animals in parked cars.

**Buses:** Local networks mostly run on routes planned for residents and commuters rather than tourists, and serve cities, counties or beach areas. Check route and times before tackling local services –

most require an exact fare. Greyhound operates interstate and serves the major cities. Cities like Miami have buses arriving almost hourly; others only have daily or weekly services, so check ahead and plan carefully.

**Rail:** Railway services are not so good in Florida. Amtrak never offers more than two services a day to any city and prices are not low enough to be attractive. Rail passes, bought before leaving home, can cut the cost. Travel agents in Europe sell both Greyhound and Amtrak tickets and can book you on specified services.

## Business Hours

Most shopping malls are open 10:00–21:00 Mon–Sat, 10:00–18:00 Sun. Other shops and offices generally open 09:00–17:00 Mon–Sat. Most offices are closed on Saturday.

## Time Difference

Florida has two time zones. Most of the state operates on Eastern Standard Time while the northwest region, west of the Apalachicola River, operates on Central Standard Time. Eastern Standard Time is five hours behind Greenwich Mean (or Universal Standard) Time (GMT) in winter, while Central Standard Time is six hours behind. Florida has United States Daylight Saving Time, advancing clocks by one hour from the last Sunday in April to the last Sunday in October.

## Communications

Postal services are generally very efficient. Stamps can be

---

<table>
<tr><td colspan="2" align="center">PUBLIC HOLIDAYS</td></tr>
</table>

**1 January** • New Year's Day
**15 January** •
Martin Luther King's Birthday
**Third Monday in February**
• Presidents Day
**March** • Good Friday
(half-day holiday)
**March** • Easter Monday
**Last Monday in May** •
Memorial Day
**4 July** • Independence Day
**First Monday in
September** • Labor Day
**Second Monday in
October** • Columbus Day
**11 November** •
Veterans Day
**Last Thursday in
November** •
Thanksgiving Day
**25 December** •
Christmas Day
Most Americans have only one day off at Christmas and Easter. Halloween (October 31) is almost a holiday with kids 'trick or treating'.

---

bought (at a small extra cost) from hotels and vending machines or at post offices. Post offices are usually open 09:00–17:00 Mon–Fri, 09:00–12:00 Sat. Post your letters in blue mailboxes on the street, in post offices or hotel lobbies. Mail to Europe takes about one week to arrive. The international telephone dialling code for the United States is 1.

Most hotels have direct dial telephones for international calls to Europe, although a credit card imprint may be required before you are allowed to use one. Phone cards are the most economical and most hotels have public call boxes. Public telephones can be found on street corners, at bars, restaurants, hotel lobbies, bus and rail stations. An automated voice will ask you to insert coins. The phone may ring immediately after you finish a call to request more money. If you do not comply, the person you called will be billed. Non-local and long-distance calls are cheaper between 18:00 and 08:00. International calls are cheapest between 23:00 and 07:00. Many tourist agencies, theme parks, attractions and car hire firms have a toll-free number (prefix 800 or 888), which can only be accessed free from inside the United States.

## Electricity

The electricity circuit runs on 110 volts, which means that equipment from many European and other countries will not work without an adaptor. The American plugs are two-pronged, but some adaptors don't fit US sockets, so you are advised to check when buying.

## Weights and Measures

All measures are imperial in the US. Petrol is bought in US gallons, which are slightly smaller than the European gallon. Clothing sizes are smaller – buy a US size 10 if you would normally wear a European size 12. For shoes, add one to the measurement (i.e. try on a size five when you would normally wear a size four).

## Health Precautions

Florida is a safe and healthy place. Water is safe to drink and food hygiene standards generally excellent. The sun is strong, so take sun cream, hats and sunglasses to avoid sunburn. If on medication, take sufficient with you – it will be available but may be more costly in Florida.

## Health Services

Health services throughout Florida are comprehensive but expensive. Make sure you are properly insured, including sufficient for repatriation if necessary. Hotels usually have a doctor on call 24 hours a day.

## Personal Safety

As in any major tourist area worldwide, tourists can become targets. A few common-sense guidelines minimize any risk:

• Do not carry large sums of cash or wear a lot of jewellery around town, at theme parks and other attractions.
• Do not walk around empty or unlit streets at night.
• Park in well-lit areas only.
• Ask for directions before leaving the hotel or airport.
• If you get lost, find a well-lit petrol station or public building to ask for assistance.
• Some rental companies offer mobile phones for use in emergencies – use them.
• If you are bumped from behind while driving, do not stop. Drive somewhere safe, then call the police if necessary.
• Do not open your hotel room door without checking who it is.
• Do not take valuables to the beach with you – keep

them in the hotel safe.
• In any emergency call **911**. The police have multilingual staff working on help lines with tourist advice.

## Emergencies

The **police**, **ambulance** and **fire service** can be contacted by dialling **911**. Companies issuing traveller's cheques may be reached on toll-free numbers in the US. Keep this number separate from your cheques and call immediately if you have lost your cheques or had them stolen. The British Consulate has an office in Miami, tel: (305) 374-1522, which you should contact if you lose your passport. Also, report stolen or lost passports or traveller's cheques to the police.

## Etiquette

Florida is a friendly place with a relaxed ambience. Dress codes are usually equally relaxed – in the evenings, however, you may want to cover up.

---

**GOOD READING**

• Brogan, Hugh (1990) *The Penguin History of the United States of America*. Penguin.
• Bryson, Bill (1996) *Made in America*. Minerva.
• Carr, Archie Fairly (1955) *Guide to the Reptiles, Amphibians and Freshwater Fishes of Florida*. FUP.
• Rawlings, Marjorie Kinnan (1992) *The Yearling*. Mammoth.
• Hemingway, Ernest (1976) *The Old Man and the Sea*. Triad; (1990) *Islands in the Stream*. Grafton.

# INDEX

Note: Numbers in **bold**
indicate photographs

## CONTENTS

CW00592076

*Dedication: When we understand more the depth of our own evil and the selfishness of all our plans, only then do we see a world reflecting his truth and designed by his perfection.*   MARK HAVILLE 2004

# LIFE'S STORY

## INTRODUCTION: The journey of life

Life is a journey, with discoveries to make, lessons to learn, and trials to overcome. For every human being, as we go through life, these things reveal to us the story of life, and in turn prompt many questions. How are we made? How did we come to be? What can we do? Is what we are now all that there will ever be of us?

Without doubt humans are the most marvellous of all the creatures that inhabit this planet. We excel through our ability to communicate by language, as well as the capacity to reason and hence to design. Our keen powers of observation have enabled us to understand the natural world around us, and using the gifts of reason we can design and produce wonderful inventions based on things seen around us: Velcro from feathers; helicopters from dragonflies; submarines from Nautilus shells – the list goes on and on. Observing the natural world has also led us to understand something of the whole universe and our part in it.

The complex world of nature and the interactions of life forms within it help us to see ways in which interdependence of one life form on another is vital to the survival of both. Scientists call this *symbiosis*, and an *ecosystem* is an environment involving a number of such interdependent life

*PuddingWife Wrasse (Halichoeres radiatus)*

forms. One question we could then ask is: If different creatures depend on each other to stay alive now, have they always done so in the past?

The discovery of the structure and importance of deoxyribonucleic acid (DNA) is one of the landmark scientific achievements of the 20th century. The DNA molecule is very complicated, but it is made up from simple chemical compounds linked in a very complex arrangement which provides a code defining the nature of every different living thing. All the information needed to build it is encoded within the molecule, but it is so tiny that an amount which covers a pinhead holds information to fill enough books to reach from the Earth to the Moon and back more than 500 times. When Charles Darwin wrote his *Origin of Species by Means of Natural Selection, or the Preservation of Favoured Races in the Struggle for Life* (complete title) 150 years ago, nothing was known of DNA. If it had been, the book might never have been published. Despite being a keen observer of natural history, Darwin refused to accept that there were fixed boundaries between the very distinct and different animal kinds. DNA research now proves this true beyond doubt, and there is no room for fanciful 'interpretation'.

**Evolutionists can only make fanciful suggestions, and further expand their theory-tale...**

Centuries of scientific observation testify to the fact that successive generations of animals are the same as their parents. As a result, supporters of the 'theory' of evolution mislead us by referring to changes in *species* as changes in *kind*. Breeders have faced these boundaries between kinds of creatures, and they know that although they can produce new species, there is a limit beyond which they cannot go. Dogs and racehorses are carefully bred to produce animals having particular qualities, but selective breeding often produces problems such as difficulty with breathing. There is one well-known example: it is possible to cross a horse with a donkey to produce a mule, but it will be almost always sterile.

So, if animal A is bred with animal B, then the offspring (animal C) can only ever be the result of a combination of

Horse with foal

the information from A and B. To become something else requires new information and new chemicals. Where would they come from? How would they become part of the process? Evolutionists can only make fanciful suggestions, and further expand their theory-tale, in the hope that the world will be convinced, but the fact remains that new *kinds* of animals can never be produced, but only variations of the *species* within the existing kinds of animals.

Continuing research on DNA has provided fascinating evidence that a mechanism exists which helps to prevent the coded information within DNA from being corrupted. When cells divide, the DNA is copied, and mistakes do occur, called mutations. These would be very destructive, but there is a code checking mechanism involving an enzyme called DNA polymerase. As new cells are formed, this checking mechanism makes sure that the information used to build each new part is exactly the same as the original. The process is rather like checking a document that has been copied against the original. DNA polymerase thus stops mutations and protects against harmful changes.

Because extra information cannot be added, when adaptations do sometimes take place, animals do not become more complex as required to support the 'theory' of macro-evolution. There is some flexibility in the DNA, but this does not go beyond allowing adaptations in size, colour and patterning. It can never result in one *kind* of animal changing into another *kind*.

> There is flexibility in the DNA...but it can never result in one kind of animal changing into another *kind*

Centuries of scientific observation testify to the stubbornness of any species of creature changing into another kind. It has been said that evolution has been 'proved' because certain types of finches can no longer breed, as ability to breed is a factor of speciation. Accepted; but this is about new species, not new kinds. Let us now go on a journey of discovery.

# CHAPTER ONE

# SYMBIOSIS

## The relationships of life

For the first stage of our journey, we will look at a coral reef and its ecosystem.

Bermuda is an island in the western Atlantic, which was discovered in 1609 by Sir George Somers. It is a volcanic island of unspoiled natural beauty. Although it has no rivers or streams it is lush, colourful and full of character. The locals affectionately call Bermuda 'God's Island', partly because of the number of times hurricanes have missed the island. It is bordered by uniquely coloured pink beaches, the sand deriving its colour from

> The sunken ships become part of the reef, being covered with brain corals, sponges and sea-fans

a small shellfish called foraminifera, and it is surrounded by clear turquoise waters, which are ideal for the formation of coral reefs. At a latitude of 32° N, Bermuda is the most northerly place on our planet where coral reefs can be found. The island is completely surrounded by them, which make it the 'shipwreck capital' of the world with around 150 wrecks littered across its reefs.

Although these waters are very dangerous to shipping, this watery world is full of variety and colour. The sunken ships become part of the reef, being covered with brain corals, sponges and sea-fans. Many of the world's reefs are in danger of extinction. Corals require clean, warm water to survive, and rapid temperature changes or severe wave action can kill corals quickly. Sand or algae smothering a reef will also kill it. Divers can also cause damage. Good coastline management and natural filters like mangrove trees help to protect reefs by forming natural barriers. These hold back sand and other sediments, which would otherwise wash down on to the reef.

In other parts of the world corals grow on outcrops of rock in the ocean. The Australian Great Barrier Reef is one example. This is so large that it can be seen from space.

Many colourful fish live in the waters of the reefs. One such fish is the Pudding Wife Wrasse. This electrically coloured fish is equipped with stereoscopic vision: the eyes can move individually and in different directions simultaneously, enabling it to form a three-dimensional image in its brain. Its pectoral fins move like oars on a rowing boat to provide precise movement control. These features are perfect for finding its favourite food.

Another reef dweller is the Butterfly fish. It has a long thin snout, which is just the right size to extract food from the grooves of the brain corals or from between the branches of the different corals. There are about 120 known species worldwide, all disc or oval shaped. They are commonly seen

*Foureye Butterfly Fish (Chaetodon capistratus)*

swimming in pairs, although some species also school. Mostly they ignore humans, only moving away when approached by a diver. They also change their colour and markings between the juvenile and adult stages, in some cases by so much that identification is difficult. They feed during the day and can also change both colour and markings at night.

Corals provide a platform for algae to grow, but overgrowth would smother the reef and the corals would die. Parrot fish, another part of the ecosystem, give valuable service by consuming algae. They do this using a strong beak perfectly made for scraping the corals. Naturalists have proposed that the fish had teeth, which evolved into the present hard beak, but it is easy to imagine what would happen to the teeth of any creature that decided to chew rocks and corals. The hard bony beak of the Parrot fish has always been as it is now, or otherwise it would have become extinct. However, the fish sometimes bites off pieces of coral whilst feeding, which is later excreted as sand. This is another example of deliberate design, as the sand produced provides a perfect environment for a host of other life forms, which are in turn needed for the survival of the fish itself as well as other creatures.

Parrot fish have some amazing features. Like many fish their scales are extremely sensitive to water pressure and movement. This means that they can swim in a shoal and never bump into each other. They can also change sex and, with this change, their colour. Such adaptability provides a greater chance of survival should large numbers of one sex be destroyed. The fish may also change colour to blend in

*Shoal of Parrot Fish*

Crab

with its surroundings; this is even more remarkable given that the fish is colour-blind.

The cycle does not stop there. An army of sea cucumbers and crustaceans clean the sand left by the Parrot fish looking for tiny particles of food. Corals and sea fans also clean the water, in order that all the aquatic life can survive. If any of these creatures were to be removed from the ecosystem, disaster would follow. Scientists used to think that the activities of Parrot fish destroyed reefs, but recent studies show that when they are excluded from feeding on an area of reef, it is quickly covered by algae and dies.

The astonishing variety of Parrot fish adds colour and variety to reefs across the world. More importantly, the symbiotic relationship of these fish raises serious questions about the origins of life. The traditional evolutionary model taught today cannot answer these questions. Coral reefs and coral reef creatures cannot survive without each other. If this is true today, is it possible that it was ever different? The logical conclusion is that they have always lived together. It is no longer the 'chicken or the egg' – Parrot fish or corals. At the microscopic level the question becomes: 'Which came first, the DNA or the enzymes?' This is the question evolutionists avoid.

> The symbiotic relationship of these fish raises serious questions about the origins of life

With our modern understanding of DNA, the changes that evolutionists postulate are seen as wishful thinking. Symbiotic relationships bring into serious question the idea that different forms of life evolved at different times. So is there further evidence to undermine this so-called 'theory'? The essence of scientific investigation is to conduct **repeatable** experiments, and only then to advance a theory. Is evolution good science? Is it really *scientism*? This is defined as an unjustified belief in the scientific method. Let us look further.

*Bottlenosedd Dolphin (Tursiops truncatus)*

# CHAPTER TWO

# CHANGES

## The lessons of life

Symbiotic relationships also stretch across environments. For example, most people would never consider that trees and other plants play a vital role in the life of dolphins. In fact, plants keep them alive, as they do humans and all other air-breathing creatures. The oxygen in the atmosphere which we all need for life is constantly being replenished by vegetation. Dolphins are air-breathers, and this means that as long as there have been dolphins, there must also have been plants.

Traditional evolutionary teaching claims that dolphins evolved from some kind of cow or some other land-based mammal. But is this really possible? Or is this 'scientific theory' really closer to 'science fiction'? To discover the truth, let us consider some of the changes that would be needed.

The dolphin breathes through a blowhole on the top of its head. This blowhole does not connect to the throat as with other mammals, which breathe through nostrils. If you have ever had water go up your nose while swimming you can understand the problem. The ability to breathe must work properly, or you would die. If an animal were evolving its nostrils into a blowhole, any intermediate stage would lead

*Bottlenosedd Dolphin*

*Bottlenosed Dolphin*

to drowning. These things cannot happen gradually. It follows that dolphins are able to feed while submerged without getting water in their lungs. However, the dolphin has consciously to close its blowhole: it is not an automatic response to diving.

The deepest recorded dive of a dolphin is 547 metres (1800 ft). The water pressure at this depth is 54 atmospheres (800 lb/sq in). Imagine the problems facing a land mammal attempting such a dive. Even human divers, with all the advanced equipment available to them, cannot reach such depths unless completely encased in a steel diving capsule.

A land-based mammal supposedly evolving to a sea-based mammal would suffer problems with vision and hearing. The eyes would have to cope with the effects of salt water, and the ears would need to adapt immediately. Divers for example can hear quite well underwater but have difficulty pinpointing the direction sounds travel from. If a diver hears a boat's engine whilst surfacing, he must visually locate the boat to ascend safely. Gradual evolutionary change could never explain how the marvellous hearing abilities of dolphins developed.

Dolphins are powerful swimmers and can easily reach speeds of more than 50 kilometres/hr (30 miles/hr). This is achieved because they have a strong muscular system built on a lightweight skeleton. They also shed the outer layer of skin cells, which contain small droplets of oil, up to twelve times a day. Thus their extremely smooth skin is constantly lubricated and provides an almost drag free surface. Most mammals have skin hair, in some cases fur, and any animal 'evolving' into a hairless form would die of cold in the sea before its body could develop the property of thermoregulation, which dolphins possess.

Reproduction is another area where dolphins differ from other mammals. The calf is born tail first because, as air breathers, the head must appear last so the baby does not have to wait to take its first breath. If it were born head first, the baby would drown before it was free to swim to the surface for air.

We can clearly see that all the adaptations needed to convert a land mammal to a sea mammal would have to happen instantly and together. Even according to evolutionists, this is a statistical impossibility. Mutations involve a loss of information. Changes of design require

Spanish Hogfish (Bodianus rufus)

**African Lionfish (Pterois mombasae)**

intelligence as well as energy, and animals simply do not have these capacities. Things do not just 'take shape'. Humans have the God-given ability to study, and then design the things they need to enter other environments, so we have boats and diving equipment to explore these underwater worlds. Can you imagine riding your bicycle on to a racing circuit in the hope that it would evolve into a Formula One racing car? Add a few million years to this fantasy, and the probability of success reduces, not increases.

Green Turtle (Chelonia mydas)

# CHAPTER THREE

# MOVEMENT

## the variety of life

The evolutionist claims that everything is continually, gradually changing. However, the fossil record only shows that the creatures still alive today have not changed in their design at all from their fossilised ancestors. If we look at this more carefully, we do find changes of size, but they are still identifiable as members of distinct family groups alive today. So if animals today are the same as their fossil ancestors, even if they could evolve, what changes in their circumstances would make them do so?

**millions of fossils have been found and catalogued, and have produced no evidence. Perhaps it's because there is none**

When Darwinian evolutionists are presented with such questions, they claim that a variety of situations which affect the survival chances of a creature will cause evolution. Factors such as predation (being eaten by something else), food supply, or climate change are examples. If, however, such things occur, how does the creature stay alive long enough to evolve? We can then ask the question: Does aquatic life show evidence of evolution?

The most significant influence on aquatic creatures is the water in which they live. Living in a watery environment, for example, significantly affects movement, but it has the same effect on all creatures. The result of this, according to the 'theory' of evolution, should be that there are only a small number of different creatures in one sea area, living under similar conditions. Let us consider the Red Sea. There are over 600 different species of fish. Many vary in the way that they move. Is it reasonable to suggest that water alone could produce so many different ways of achieving the same goals? And even if different conditions existed at some time in the past, which produced a large number of different fish, why are 600 of them still alive today and surviving in an identical environment? Could this be evidence that they did not evolve to begin with?

As an example, consider the various species of puffer fish. They all have an inflexible skeleton, and are propelled by their fins and tails alone. The only other part of the body which moves is the mouth. The other fish all have flexible spines – why did they 'evolve' in such a different way from everything else?

Parrot fish have been mentioned already. Their movement is precisely controlled using pectoral and tail fins.

Flat fish have a hovering motion, rather like a 'magic carpet'. At first glance it is difficult to imagine them moving quickly enough to avoid danger, but they can move very quickly when necessary.

The graceful and mysterious manta ray appears almost to

Emperor Penguins (aptenodytes porsteri)

*Smooth Trunkfish (Lactophrys triqueter)*

*Long Spined Sea Urchin*

be flying under water. Eels move rather like snakes, winding from side to side.

The octopus jets itself forward by forcing water through a siphon and using its eight legs for extra propulsion. The turtle, despite being a heavy creature, moves gracefully through the ocean. Its streamlined shell reduces drag, whilst its flippers slice through the water giving effortless movement. Shrimps, lobsters and crayfish all use their legs to walk across the sea bed as well as across rocks and corals. Their extremely strong tails provide sudden thrust, up to 150 kilometres/hr (90 miles/hr) in some species, helping them to escape danger.

No matter how these varied creatures move under water, they all move perfectly and without effort. Therefore the suggestion that there was a common ancestor cannot be true. The challenge to evolutionists is to prove their own assertions, and to answer our questions. Why do

**Spotted Moray
(Gymnothorax moringa)**

fossils not show any change. Why hasn't palaeontology, after 150 years of trying, produced one 'intermediate' fossil? After all, millions of fossils have been found and catalogued, and have produced no evidence. Perhaps it's because there is none. If this is so why is the unproven "theory" of evolution still taught in our schools and colleges?

Mahsena Emperor (*Lethrinus mahsena*)

# CHAPTER FOUR

# DESTINY
## the meaning of life

Evolutionists try to separate science from world views or philosophy because they say that religion is not science and vice versa. This is both unnecessary and dishonest. If the Bible says that the Earth is round and hangs in space, which it does, do we ignore this correct statement because it comes from a religious source? Should we not test every 'scientific' sounding statement by proven scientific methods? Recent discoveries through scientific experiments further call into question the 'theory' that chemicals could evolve into living organisms. The

> No theory of evolution can be formed to account for the similarity of molecules, for evolution necessarily implies continuous change

truth is that modern man, as the Bible predicted thousands of years ago, has become more arrogant, suppressing any evidence showing that life on Earth originates from a divine source.

An evolutionist biology professor at Kansas State

University stated: '... even if all the data points to an intelligent designer, such an idea is excluded from science because it is not naturalistic.' This kind of statement is *not* scientific, nor even intellectually honest. It is *scientism*. Throughout history, some of the most notable scientists have publicly acknowledged that the processes witnessed in nature in no way contradicted their Christian faith. True science agrees with the Bible, and many of them were aided in their research by building on the foundation of biblical truth. All other religious books, including the Book of Mormon, the Qur'an, the Bhagavadgita, together with the writings of many self-proclaimed prophets, contain scientifically absurd statements. In contrast, some of the world's most brilliant minds have come from a Judaeo-

*Striped Butterfly fish (Chaetodon Fasciatus)*

*Shy Hamlet (Hypoplectrus guttavavarius)*

Christian background, including Sir Isaac Newton, Lord Kelvin and James Maxwell. These quotes are just examples.

Sir Isaac Newton (discovered the laws of motion and gravity): 'Atheism is so senseless. When I look at the solar system, I see the Earth at the right distance from the Sun to receive the proper amount of heat and light. This did not happen by chance.'

Lord Kelvin (discovered the first two laws of thermodynamics): 'Overwhelmingly strong proofs of intelligent design lie around us ... the atheistic idea is so non-sensical that I cannot put it into words.'

James Maxwell (discovered electromagnetic field equations): ' No theory of evolution can be formed to account for the similarity of molecules, for evolution

*Scalefin Anthias (Pseudanthias squamipinnis)*

*Steephead Parrotfish (Scarus gibbus)*

necessarily implies continuous change … the exact equality of each molecule to all others of the same kind gives it … the essential character of a manufactured article.'

Words of wisdom from such scholarly men as these could be multiplied again and again. Therefore to reject the 'theory' of evolution is not to be unscientific in our view of the natural history of this wonderful world.

*Sergeant Majors (Abudefduf vaigensis)*

Lion (Panthera Leo)

# CHAPTER FIVE

# SPECIES
## the facts of life

We will now continue our journey. Africa, the land of safaris, is a continent full of variety and beauty, but our focus is on one remarkable bird: the ostrich.

Ostriches are the 'camels' of the bird family. They are able to survive for months without food by using oil stored in their bodies, and more than five weeks without water. Most of the water they need is produced internally, the rest is obtained from the vegetation they eat. The female is therefore able to sit on her eggs and guard them for the forty days' incubation period. The eggs have been

**Is the history of life unclear, or is it now being presented in a way which only fits an evolutionary model?**

specially designed for ground nesting, with shells strong enough to take the weight of a full-grown man. Do not try stealing her eggs – she could chase you for thirty minutes at 40mph, and still be able to deliver a lethal kick! In any case, the eggs take over two hours to boil.

The native bushmen use the eggs to store water by making a small hole in the top, filling it and burying it. They will then retrieve it on their return from a hunting trip, even finding it in trackless desert.

One puzzling feature of the ostrich is that it has wings but cannot fly. However, they are important as air brakes, and are also used for air conditioning. Most birds have natural oil in their feathers for waterproofing, but ostrich feathers lack this oil. The feathers are thus ideal for keeping cool as well as retaining heat, which is very necessary in desert conditions, where scorching mid-day temperatures can fall to 14 F (−10 C) at night. Each feather has a distinctive white pattern which, like a human fingerprint, is unique. This has no evolutionary value, but simply highlights the limitless creative ability of a Master Designer.

Ostriches have the strongest immune system known to man, and are among the healthiest creatures in the world. Despite this, eventually death comes, as it does to every

*Male Ostrich (Struthio Camelus)*

creature. Death is one of life's greatest mysteries – all animal and vegetable matter must die sooner or later, whether the strongest or the weakest. This is something we all have to face.

One thing is certain: Ostriches have only ever produced ostriches. An examination of the fossil record shows this is true of the past, and simple observation of the present shows it is still true. So we can ask ourselves whether the past is really so mysterious. Does it have to be somehow different from that which we can see today? Or does the present teach clear

*Female Ostrich (Struthio Camelus)*

lessons about the unchanging nature of life?

Is the history of life unclear, or is it now being presented in a way which only fits an evolutionary model? If so, why? If there is good evidence that all creation was designed, then what does this suggest about our final destiny? Do we share an ancestor with apes, or were we designed and created in the image of God? There are similarities between apes and humans, as well as with other forms of life, but what about the differences? Are these differences being ignored because they do not fit the model postulated by the 'theory' of evolution?

If the answer to all these questions points to a Master Designer, then there are profound implications for every man, woman and child.

*Nanday Conure (Nandayas nenday)*

# CHAPTER SIX

# ADAPTATIONS

## the facts of life

Let us now look at some other remarkable animals to be seen on an African safari. These creatures will show us more of the wonderful design that is evident throughout all creation.

Wildebeest roam the vast plains in large herds, continually migrating to get the best food supply. This constant movement allows grass to grow again. Their long front legs and sloping backs help them to conserve energy on long journeys. These journeys also reduce their chances of becoming prey to lions and other predators.

> the fossil record shows no evidence of the wildebeest ever having been other than it now is

A wildebeest calf is able to run and keep up with the herd within an hour of birth. The cow possesses a unique regulatory system to control the moment when the afterbirth is excreted, and it will not be discharged until the calf can run with the herd. The cow will lead her calf well away from that place, because the smell of blood attracts predators. The wildebeest is the only antelope to possess this amazing ability. This clearly shows that it did not evolve from any

*Wildebeest (Connochaetes Taurinus)*

other mammal, and nothing else has evolved from it. In addition, the fossil record shows no evidence of the wildebeest ever having been other than it now is.

The wildebeest is naturally very cautious, but will graze alongside other antelopes, ostriches and zebra, but will flee from predators, because it knows the difference. How?

Giraffes also have unique features. Most mammals give birth lying down, but the giraffe is vulnerable when lying down, as it takes some time to get to its feet and would be easy prey. To compensate, it delivers the calf standing up, and her unique features allow safe birth, even though the calf has to drop six feet to the ground. First to emerge are the long hind legs, helping to break the fall. The afterbirth stays attached to the cow and thus acts like an elastic rope helping to lower it gently to the ground. Also, the calf's neck is designed to fold back along the body so that it can take its first breath more quickly. The evolutionist cannot explain any of these features.

The giraffe feeds on the leaves of an acacia called the Knob Thorn, using its prehensile tongue to take leaves from between the thorns, which are very long, tough and extremely sharp. The pollen from the flowers rubs off on their necks, which helps to pollinate other trees, as they travel up to nine miles a day in search of food, giving another example of symbiosis.

The Bible tells us that thorns are part of the curse that God put on the Earth because of Adam's sin. We can see a reflection of this curse in the way that the Lord Jesus had a crown of thorns (likely to be from such a tree) forced on his head before he was crucified. Predation is also a result of the curse.

**The more we study the marvels of nature, the more we have to challenge the validity of evolutionary thinking**

The lion is a formidable hunter. It can run at 35 mph (55kph), leap 40ft (12m) and jump 12ft (3.5m), even though it weighs 275 – 450 lb (125-200kg), equivalent to 80–130 tabby cats! It can measure up to nine feet (2.75m) from nose to tail. Its roar, a unique property of large cats, can be more than 100 decibels in loudness and can be heard up to five miles (8km) away. It has a territorial purpose, both to attract members of the pride and warn off other lions.

Male African Lion (Panthera Leo)

The male lion is the only member of the cat family to have a mane. There is much debate as to its function. Did God create it to attract females, or simply because it pleased him to give the male lion extra glory? There is some evidence to suggest the former. The pattern of whiskers on the muzzle is unique, like a human fingerprint, giving further evidence of individuality within similarity.

For the most part, lions are meat-eaters, their diet normally including zebra, wildebeest, antelopes and baby giraffe. Smaller prey is killed with a bite to the back of the neck, severing the spinal column, or by breaking the neck with a blow from its powerful paw. Larger prey is suffocated or strangled with a bite to the throat. However, they can survive on a totally vegetarian diet, as was proved during World War Two, when zoo lions were only fed vegetables

African Elephant (Loxodonta africana)

because meat was rationed. Baby lions are, however, just like other mammals and feed on mother's milk. Only later will they be weaned and start feeding on meat.

Where do these facts lead us? The more we study the marvels of nature, the more we have to challenge the validity of evolutionary thinking. In this chapter, the evidence leads us to a number of questions, such as:

Why do wildebeest have such a body shape?

How did wildebeest and giraffes develop such unusual birth processes?

How do wildebeest know predatory animals?

Where did the prehensile tongue of the giraffe come from?

Why does the lion have a 'whisker fingerprint'?

Why does a baby lion prefer its mother's milk to grass or meat?

How does any animal mother know how to care for her young?

Underlying these questions are more fundamental concepts, particularly the role of DNA in the production of succeeding generations and the significance of the non-physical aspects of creatures. Even if creatures *could* evolve from other creatures, how did the non-physical aspects, such as reason and emotion in humans, and instincts in animals first appear? If humans evolved from apes (a common claim), how did we lose our ape-like instincts and need to be taught almost everything? Humans are not just clever apes; we did not evolve from them.

> If humans evolved from apes, how did we lose our ape-like instincts and need to be taught almost everything?

Evolutionists always focus on the similarities between animals and humans, and conveniently ignore the great differences which exist, not only between animals and humans but also between different kinds of animals.

The DNA code for each life form contains billions of bits of information. Hence a small percentage variation from one form to another is still a large figure, amounting to millions of bits. We hear a great deal about the similarities between apes and humans (98% of DNA), but the differences clearly show that a common link is impossible. Apes would need a complete redesign of their hip structures

Chacma Baboon (Papio ursinus)

to walk upright and while this change was evolving the creature would be unable to walk. This is just one of many changes that would be involved if we were to assume that evolution is true.

Much has been made of the idea that birds developed from reptiles. It is easy to see that scales are unlike feathers, and feathers are unlike fur, but what are the differences? Each is made from different materials, and hence for a creature to make the change it would need a new DNA code. Where would this come from? Even if there were a way to obtain the materials, a new DNA 'blueprint' would be needed for the new structures, and existing body parts would have to be redesigned to accommodate the changes. This is effectively making something out of nothing, rather than adapting what was already there. Evolutionists are fond of saying: 'We believe that (so and so) then happened', but produce no *scientific* evidence of change. Evolution is therefore exposed as a system of beliefs, rather than a fully worked out scientific theory.

We have seen that adaptations can only produce new species which are variations of the existing. The new species is a mixture of the parent stock, a rearrangement of the existing information, not a new *kind*. The highly specialised attributes of the animals we have looked at show no sign of changing, and successive generations look and behave just like their parents.

> Evolutionists are fond of saying: 'We believe that (so and so) then happened', but produce no *scientific* evidence of change

What about behaviour? This is a non-physical matter which is not coded into DNA but which is vital to survival in the world of nature. Animals are born with instincts, knowledge if you will, and use this to survive and rear their young. Some animals appear to learn part of their necessary behaviour from parents, while others learn none. The lessons derived from their own experience of life would never be enough for them to acquire survival skills. Death would be inevitable. There would be no time for evolution to help them. Humans are different. We have to be taught almost everything. In this important aspect, we are very different from animals. A deeper question needs to be asked of evolutionists – how could these non-physical attributes evolve?

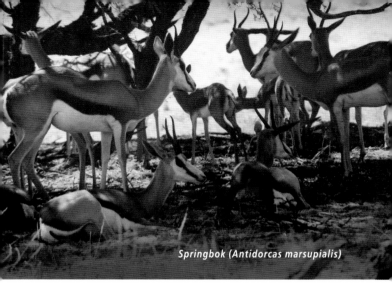
*Springbok (Antidorcas marsupialis)*

We have seen how the giraffe gets its food from a thorn tree. According to the Bible, thorns are one result of the curse that God placed upon creation following Adam's sin. This is also the reason why everything in creation dies physically and non-living things are subject to decay. The Bible says that man returns to the dust from which he was created, and we are reminded of this truth each time the house is cleaned, because household dust contains about 85% human skin particles.

Everything about life makes sense when we know how it all began. Honest study of the life around us leads to the creator of all life. It is very sad that so many would rather believe the theory-tale of evolution, simply because they do not want to admit that there is a God who has created everything.

# CHAPTER SEVEN

# IRREDUCIBILITY
## The complexity of life

It is possible to show scientifically that something has been designed by applying the principle of irreducible complexity. This simply means that a series of related functioning parts of a system must all work together and at the same time or it will not work at all. A bicycle is a simple example. The proof that it is a designed article lies in the fact that the frame, wheels cogs and chain must all be in place and working at the same time, or the bicycle will not work. It would be impossible for each component to evolve separately and gradually. In addition, each component must be designed and made to the right size to fit with the rest. This shows that a bicycle is a product of intelligence and energy, not chance.

In Africa, created animals show the same properties. Even animals within the same family group (or kind) have unique abilities and differences. The Kalahari wildcat needs speed and cunning to catch a mouse, and winds itself up like a spring before it pounces. Hunger is the instinct that gives this pattern of behaviour: humans know this same feeling, but how could it have evolved 'gradually'?

The black-backed jackal also uses its tail, but usually to communicate with other members of the pack. Jackals are both hunters and scavengers, cleaning up waste meat which

Giraffe (Giraffa Camelopardalis)

would rot and spread disease. This is an important symbiotic function in this ecosystem.

The cheetah is smaller than the lion or the leopard, but it hunts with similar skills. It is the fastest of the big cats, and has tremendous acceleration. One was observed chasing off a rival for about a mile (1.5km) at 65 mph (100kph); more usually it will run at around 45 mph (70kph) for distances of about 450yds (400metres) before resting. Its acceleration is greater than a powerful sports car. These bursts of speed are possible because it has larger nasal passages than other big cats, and can maintain a good supply of oxygen to its lungs. Its spine is more flexible and legs proportionately longer, its body size to weight ratio is greater, and its feet can grip the ground better at high speeds than other big cats. It can also use its tail for balance and to assist turning at high speed.

> The other important fact is that only life can produce life, and only of the same kind

Compared with the lion or leopard, its teeth are smaller. Larger nasal passages means it only has room for the roots of small teeth. If cheetahs once had large teeth and large nasal cavities, their teeth would have fallen out during feeding time. The jawbone, nasal passages and teeth must be designed together. This is another example of irreducible complexity: all such things require a designer, an input of knowledge and energy in a perfectly controlled manner.

*Cheetah (Acinonyx jubatur)*

Cheetah cubs weigh less than those of the other big cats and are born much more quickly. Thus pregnancy does not impair the cheetah's ability to run and hunt.

The mammalian knee joint is an extremely good example of irreducible complexity, whether we look at the cheetah or the human knee. Two bones move over each other, controlled by muscles and ligaments. Two very important ligaments are known as the cruciate ligaments. These pass from the back to the front of the knee through a recess in the bones, crossing over as they do so, thus providing lateral stability to the joint. Sportsmen who damage this vital component soon find out that this injury is painful, disabling and very difficult to repair. Suffice to say these components of the

Cheetah's paws

knee are irreducible mechanisms, and are vital one to another. All must all be in place at the same time. Kneeling before someone has always represented humility and penitence. No wonder our creator put a cross in our knees.

The facts given in this chapter all lead us to an inevitable conclusion. Nature must have had a designer. The immense periods of time required to fit in with evolutionary ideas would mean almost certain extinction for species of creatures in the period during which change disabled them from functioning properly. The other important fact is that only life can produce life, and only of the same kind.

Simple observations and scientific deductions from them lead us to wonder how honest scientists can still embrace evolutionary ideas. Understanding of these things has developed so much in the 150 years or so since Darwin published *Origin of Species*, but still many people (including scientists) cling to an unsupportable set of views based on that book. None of them, however, can support their ideas with scientifically based experimental evidence, or from anything observed in nature.

*Pair of cheetahs*

# CHAPTER EIGHT

# ETERNITY

## The continuation of life

For the last chapter of this book we turn to another source of knowledge about our origins; the Bible. Who created our world? How was it done?

The Bible is clear. In the book of Genesis (this word means 'beginnings') it states plainly in its opening words: 'In the beginning God created the heaven and the earth.' (Genesis 1:1). Time and again in this first chapter we read the words: 'And God said': 'And God made': 'And God called'. God created all life simply by speaking it into existence. He then brought every creature before Adam (the first man) to name. It was a gloriously complex creation, all its facets interlinking and working together for their mutual good. This chapter also tells us that 'God saw that it was good'.

> Words are language, and language only comes from an intelligent source

Words are language, and language only comes from an intelligent source. Recent DNA research reveals that the very building blocks of life contain an invisible language. This coded language is baffling to science: it is nevertheless there.

Giant Tortoise (Geochelone nigra)

The supporters of the evolutionary view are actually promoting atheism and humanism, dishonestly hiding behind a smokescreen of pursuing 'scientific truth.' The various world religions are only looking for their version of truth. But we all know that truth, eternal truth, is not something physical – it is outside our physical experiences, and does not change with time or circumstances.

When he was on earth, Jesus said 'the words that I speak unto you, they are spirit, and they are life.' (John 6:63). How can words be spiritual, and how can they give life? The answer is also given in the Bible. The book of Hebrews says; 'Through faith we understand that the worlds were made by the word of God, so that things which are seen were not made of things which do appear.' (Hebrews 11:3). So faith in God and in his word (the Bible) is the key which unlocks these mysteries. It also lends new meaning to our understanding of the atomic structure of matter – there is a great deal of space inside a lump of iron! Truly all our discoveries are covered by more words from the Bible: 'there is no new thing under the sun.' (Ecclesiastes 1:9). Everything we see around us is made of invisible components.

> eternal truth, is not something physical – it is outside our physical experiences, and does not change with time or circumstances

Blacksmith (*Lapwing Venelius armatus*)

We also know that all matter in the universe is decaying, both living and non-living. This process is known to scientists as entropy. Iron rusts, rocks erode, and all living things die eventually. Recently, a lady aged 105 died in England. The doctor knew of no disease that she was suffering from, so had simply to write 'Old Age' on the death certificate. We can only say that all matter must have had a beginning. In order for there to be a start, there had to be an eternal creator to make the start. So something that is not physical and outside time (i.e. eternal) must have made all that ever existed.

Emotions and thoughts are also a part of the invisible life within us, a reflection of the intelligent, invisible God that made us, and whose words give life. Again Jesus, the Son of God, said: 'I am the way, the truth, and the life: no man

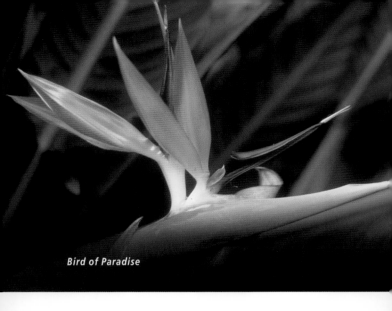

*Bird of Paradise*

cometh unto the Father, but by me.' This is another way by which we can understand the eternal character of the creator God.

But why do we need to believe these things? What difference will it make? The Bible answers these questions as well. It tells us that God is infinitely pure and holy and that he hates sin—a word not often heard today, which simply means doing those things which are wrong in God's sight. The Bible also makes clear that 'doing' includes 'thinking' and 'saying'.

The standard of measurement God has given is found in Exodus 20. The Ten Commandments, written in modern English, say:

You will not have any God except the one true God.

*Masked Weaver Bird (Ploceus velatus)*

You will not make idols, statues or images of gods or created things or worship such things, nor bow down to them.

You will not use God's name vainly (i.e. blasphemy).

You will keep one day in each week free from all works and used only for God.

You will honour and respect your parents.

You will not commit murder.

You will not have sexual relationships outside marriage (of one man to one woman).

You will not steal.

You will not tell lies.

You will not desire the possessions of others.

This is God's standard of goodness. If you have **never**

**Repentance is turning away from ourselves and towards God**

broken any of these commandments (including in your deepest thoughts), then you do not need God's salvation. Sadly, none of us can say this, but the Bible also promises a new eternal life to those who are truly sorry before God for all their sins, and put their faith only in Jesus Christ, who died on the cross and returned to life on the third day, and has the power, as God, to forgive **all** our sins. In essence, sin is what we are, even our thoughts. Repentance is turning away from ourselves and towards God.

God has provided a wealth of evidences for the truth and reliability of the Bible. One method among many is to look at its many prophecies. For example, there are over three hundred prophecies about Jesus Christ, all written centuries before he came. These foretell where he would be born, how he would live his life, details of his perfect nature and even of his death by crucifixion 400 years before the Romans devised this brutal method of execution. It was also foretold that he would raise himself from the dead. These prophecies were fulfilled in every detail during his life on earth, and there is plenty of evidence from outside the Bible of this. It is not theory or fantasy, but facts. He is God and alive today, proving he is the only Saviour of mankind.

So now you know *Life's Story*. God designed the universe by his infinite wisdom. He spoke it into existence by his power, and we see this through his wonderful creation in this

Jesus Thorn Tree

world. He has decreed that his glorious presence will be the eternal home of all those who believe in him, having been saved from condemnation by the work of his eternal Son, Jesus Christ.

Our bodies must die one day. Even a healthy lady of 105 had to die. That part of us which is non-physical will spend eternity somewhere outside the limitations of physical matter; heaven or hell.

The choice has to be made before death—there is no possibility of change after death, despite what is sometimes taught. Most of us are aware of what we call our 'shortcomings', but the Bible calls such things 'sins'. Some of us try to 'do better next time' but in the depths of our consciences we know this is a hopeless task. What is needed is a complete change, and this only God can do through his Spirit working within us. The prophet Isaiah called to his countrymen the Israelites: 'Seek the Lord while he may be found, call upon him while he is near…' (Isaiah 55:6). Confess your sins to him, repent and believe in the Lord Jesus Christ. That will give you true joy and peace, whatever life may throw at you.

'Therefore if any man be in Christ, he is a new creature; old things are passed away; behold, all things are become new.' (2 Corinthians 5:17)

Black Hornbill (*Anthracoceros malayanus*)

## About the author

Mark Haville is married to Melanie and they have six children, Inna, Kirsty, Daniel, Hannah, Samuel and Joshua. Together they run NPN VIDEOS, a ministry producing and distributing Christian media. Their high quality and biblically based programmes are already winning awards and being televised around the world.

---

### Life's Story Video/DVD available

For information about where you can obtain copies of this superb presentation, go to www.christianvideos.co.uk or call 07000 073 373

*'The photography is breathtaking, the science is crystal clear and the application is thoroughly Biblical. Life's Story is surely a contender for Best in its Class! I commend it wholeheartedly.'* **Dr John Blanchard**

---

© Day One Publications 2004   First printed 2004

All Scripture quotations are taken from the **Authorized Version**

A CIP record is held at The British Library       ISBN 1 903087 71 6

Published by Day One Publications  Ryelands Road, Leominster, HR6 8NZ

☎ 01568 613 740  FAX 01568 611 473   email—sales@dayone.co.uk  www.dayone.co.uk

Chief Sub editor: David Simm

Photography by: Christopher Hugges, Jacques Groenewald, Mark Haville

Design and Art Direction: Steve Devane   Printed by CPD